ROBERT BURNS was born in Alloway on 25 January 1759 and died in Dumfries aged 37 on 21 July 1796. He is Scotland's National Poet and probably the world's favourite poet, and wrote hundreds of poems and songs, mainly in Scots. He also collected folk songs from all over Scotland, and often revised them or based new work on them. At the age of 27 he published *Poems, Chiefly in the Scottish Dialect*, the only book of his poetry published during his short lifetime.

JOHN CAIRNEY, actor, writer, painter and lecturer, grew up in Glasgow. He became a household name when he played Robert Burns on the small screen in the 1960s, and became known as 'the Face of Burns'. He has published many books on Burns and other subjects. He lives with his wife, the actress and writer Alannah O'Sullivan, in Glasgow.

CLARK McGINN was born and bred in Ayr and walked the same streets as Rabbie when growing up. From his first Burns Supper performance at Ayr Academy to an international speaking programme proposing the Immortal Memory in many countries every year, he is a well known after dinner speaker and writer (combined with a day job in a major UK bank). For the 250th anniversary in 2009 he is deeply honoured to have been asked to give the eulogy to Burns at the commemoration service at Poets' Corner in Westminster Abbey.

BOB DEWAR was born in Edinburgh and published his first illustrations at the age of 16. He went on to ghost Dennis the Menace and to work on *The Scotsman*. He has since illustrated many books, worked for many newspapers, held exhibitions and had caricatures hung in the House of Commons, among other places.

POEMS,

CHIEFLY IN THE

SCOTTISH DIALECT,

BY

ROBERT BURNS.

Illustrations by
BOB DEWAR,
with an Introduction by
JOHN CAIRNEY,
and an Afterword by
CLARK McGINN.

KILMARNOCK EDITION:

PUBLISHED BY THE LUATH PRESS.

MM,XV.

First published 1786: Subscriber Edition of 612 copies

The Luath Kilmarnock Edition first published 2009:
Subscriber Edition of 612 copies
ISBN 978-1-906817-08-4

Trade hardback edition 2009
ISBN 978-1-906307-67-7

Trade paperback edition 2015
ISBN 978-1-910021-51-4

Reprinted 2016
ISBN 978-1-910745-74-8

Reprinted 2017, 2018

The paper used in this book is sourced from
renewable forestry and is FSC credited material.

Printed and bound by
Bell & Bain Ltd., Glasgow

Design by Tom Bee

Typeset in Mrs Eaves by 3btype.com

THE Simple Bard, unbroke by rules of Art,
He pours the wild effusions of the heart:
And if inspir'd, 'tis Nature's pow'rs inspire;
Her's all the melting thrill, and her's the
    kindling fire.

ANONYMOUS

CONTENTS

PREFACE

THE FOLLOWING TRIFLES are not the production of the Poet, who, with all the advantages of learned art, and perhaps amid the elegancies and idlenesses of upper life, looks down for a rural theme, with an eye to Theocrítes or Virgil. To the Author of this, these and other celebrated names their contrymen are, in their original languages, 'A fountain shut up, and a 'book sealed.' Unacquainted with the necessary requisítes for commencing Poet by rule, he sings the sentiments and manners, he felt and saw in himself and his rustic compeers around him, in his and their native language. Though a Rhymer from his earliest years, at least from the earliest impulses of the softer passions, ít was not till very lately, that the applause, perhaps the partialíty, of Friendship, wakened his vaníty so far as to make him think any thing of his was worth showing; and none of the following works were ever composed with a view to the press. To amuse himself with the líttle creations of his own fancy, amid the toil and fatigues of a laborious life; to transcribe the various feelings, the loves, the griefs, the hopes, the fears, in his own breast; to find some kind of counterpoise to the struggles of a world, always an alien scene, a task uncouth to the poetical mind; these were his motives for courting the Muses, and in these he found Poetry to be ít's own reward.

Now that he appears in the public character of an Author, he does it with fear and trembling. So dear is fame to the rhyming tribe, that even he, an obscure, nameless Bard, shrinks aghaſt, at the thought of being branded as 'An impertinent blockhead, obtruding his nonsense on the world; and because he can make a shift to jingle a few doggerel, Scotch rhymes together, looks upon himself as a Poet of no small consequence forsooth.'

It is an observation of that celebrated Poet,* whose divine Elegies do honor to our language, our nation, and our species, that 'Humiliſty has depressed many a genius to a hermit, but never raised one to fame.' If any Critic catches at the word *genius*, the Author tells him, once for all, that he certainly looks upon himself as poſſeſt of some poetic abiliſties, otherwise his publishing in the manner he has done, would be a manœuvre below the worſt character, which, he hopes, his worſt enemy will ever give him: but to the genius of a Ramsay, or the glorious dawnings of the poor, unfortunate Ferguson, he, with equal unaffected sincerity, declares, that, even in his higheſt pulse of vanity, he has not the moſt diſtant pretensions. These two juſtly admired Scotch Poets he has often had in his eye in the following pieces; but rather with a view to kindle at their flame, than for servile imiſtation.

* Shenſtone

To his Subscribers, the Author returns his most sincere thanks. Not the mercenary bow over a counter, but the heart-throbbing gratitude of the Bard, conscious how much he is indebted to Benevolence and Friendship, for gratifying him, if he deserves it, in that dearest wish of every poetic bosom—to be distinguished. He begs his readers, particularly the Learned and the Polite, who may honor him with a perusal, that they will make every allowance for Education and Circumstances of Life: but, if after a fair, candid, and impartial criticism, he shall stand convicted of Dulness and Nonsense, let him be done by, as he would in that case do by others—let him be condemned, without mercy, to contempt and oblivion.

CONTEMPORARY CRITICAL RESPONSES TO
THE KILMARNOCK EDITION*

There is a pathos and delicacy in his serious poems; a vein of wit and humour in those of a more festive turn which cannot be too much admired, nor too warmly approved; and I think I shall never open the book without feeling my astonishment renewed and increased.

THOMAS BLACKLOCK, poet, September 1786

The author is indeed a striking example of native genius bursting through the obscurity of poverty and the obstructions of laborious life... His observations on human characters are acute and sagacious, and his descriptions are lively and just. Of rustic pleasantry he has a rich fund; and some of his softer scenes are touched with inimitable delicacy.

Edinburgh Magazine, October 1786

He appears to be not only a keen satirist, but a man of great feeling and sensibility.

Letter by 'ALLAN RAMSAY', Edinburgh Evening Courant, 13 November 1786

... a genius of no ordinary rank... readers... will discover a high tone of feeling, a power and energy of expression...

HENRY MACKENZIE, Lounger, 9 December 1786

His simple strains, artless and unadorned, seem to flow without effort from the native feelings of the heart. They are always nervous, sometimes inelegant, often natural, simple and sublime... his verses are sometimes struck off with a delicacy, and artless simplicity, that charms like the bewitching though irregular touches of a Shakespear.

JAMES ANDERSON, Monthly Review, December 1786

... elegant, simple and pleasing.

New Annual Register, 1787

a natural, *though not a* legitimate, *son of the muses.*

JOHN LOGAN, English Review, February 1787

...we do not recollect to have ever met with a more signal instance of true and uncultivated genius, than in the author of these Poems.

Critical Review, May 1787

* *Robert Burns: The Critical Heritage*, ed. Donald A. Low (Routledge, 1974)

A NOTE FROM THE PUBLISHERS

All italicisation, capitalisation and elision from the original Kilmarnock Edition have been retained in this edition. No attempt has been made to correct or modernise spelling and punctuation from the original, though for the benefit of modern readers, ſ and ſſ have been replaced by s and ss.

INTRODUCTION

THERE ARE SOME events in the Scottish Story which are considered significant by all Scots. The Battle of Bannockburn in 1314 and the Declaration of Arbroath in 1320 are two of the earlier dates in Scotland's historical calendar, although most Scots today tactfully forget that the latter was addressed to the Pope of the time. More shameful dates from our past were the Darien Disaster of 1699 when the Scots colony in Panama was allowed to starve by the English fleet and the Union of Parliaments in 1707 when the same England bought Scotland at a bargain price for some pieces of gold. Scotland had to wait until 1928 for revenge when the Wembley Wizards thrashed England 5–1. Nearly 40 years later, the Scots of Hamilton sent young Winnie Ewing to Parliament as a Scottish Nationalist and, not long afterwards, Jimmy Reid and his fellow shipbuilders cocked a Clydebank snook at Downing Street and London rule. These were heady times for the re-awakened sense of Scottish identity, but one vital Scottish date remains obscure, and yet it's as important to our sense of Scotland now as any of the above. I refer to 31 July 1786 which was the publication date of the first, and only, book of poems published by Robert Burns of Ayr.

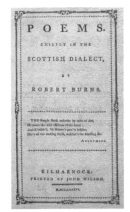

It is surely unique in any country that a poet should take his place among the pantheon of national heroes, like the swordbearers, Bruce, Wallace and General Gordon, the explorers, Mungo Park and Livingstone, the great minds, Clerk Maxwell, Napier and Hume, the inventors, Simpson, Graham Bell and Logie Baird and the scorers of goals like R.S. McColl, Jimmy McGrory and Denis Law. Yet to Scots everywhere, those of Scots descent and those who wish they were Scots, Robert Burns speaks still for our status as a nation and for our individual dignity as part of a specific people. Burns never ever said that Scots were a superior race, anything but. However, he did hold that at our best we were equal to any. In his verse and song, his essential message was supra-national, truly inter-national. Robert Burns is global and his work touches all peoples. And whether we like it or not, he tells us to celebrate our oneness, for, as he insists, we are as fellow creatures under a common Maker, whatever we call Him — or Her.

Thanks to the efforts of his Masonic brethren in Ayrshire throughout 1785 and 1786, Burns first spoke to the world as a summer voice coming out of the sun to dazzle his fellow-Masons and local compatriots with *Poems, Chiefly in the Scottish Dialect*, 612 copies of which issued from John Wilson's Print Shop at the Star Close on the corner of King Street, Kilmarnock. Rumour has it 618 copies were actually put out and the extra six given to Burns as author's copies as he couldn't afford to buy them. That may be, but ît is on record that Gilbert Burns took orders at Mossgiel for 70 copies. The method of funding was by subscription and Burns had 96 sheets of proposals printed which announced 'Scotch Poems by Robert Burns' as a heading and left room for intending purchasers to append their names as a promise to buy. When friends had gathered enough names on paper, and the printing coſts covered, only then did the selected poems go to John Wilson. Burns was lucky in his friends. One of whom, incidentally, the lawyer Robert Aiken, bought 145 to diſtribute among friends. Indeed, the whole print-run was bought out by 'sons of old Killie, assembled by Willie', as Burn's *Masonic Song* of 1786 has ît. These nine gentlemen were all members of the Kilmarnock Kilwinning Lodge under Major Will Parker. They were Tam Samson, Robert Muir, John Goldie, Gavin Turnbull, Baillie Greenshields and three medical doctors, Moore, Hamilton and Paterson. Poet Burns was made an honorary member of their lodge, being the firſt public geſture of approval he had been given and also the firſt time he had been called Poet. All Burnsians owe much to Freemasonry for the creating of Scotland's national Bard.

And similarly to Kilmarnock, for ît was in Ayrshire's capîtal that the book that made his name firſt emerged, causing a minor earthquake, firſt at the parish level, then at diſtrict and county level until finally the reverberations were country-wide and the world beckoned. To this day, Kilmarnock remains the epicentre of that 18th century midsummer explosion that was this little book of 240 pages. The town remains the home of The Robert Burns World Federation Limited, founded in 1885 as the Burns Federation, with headquarters in the grounds of Dean Castle. This original link with the poet gives Kilmarnock the right to claim its place as the wellspring of the writer, Burns, and the hub from which all writing on him should spoke out around the rim of the world. Yet Burns himself was almost diffident, albeit grateful for the impact his couple of dozen uneven pieces had produced. However, the overall effect was sensational, and astounding for a young rural rhymer. As he said himself in his autobiographical letter to Dr Moore in 1787:

> I weighed my productions as impartially as is in my power; I thought they had merit; and 'twas a delicious idea that I should be thought a clever fellow, even though it should never reach my ears, a poor negro driver, or perhaps a victim to that inhospitable clime gone to the world of the spirits. I can only say that as a pauvre inconnu, as I then was, I had as nearly as high opinion of myself and my works as I have at this moment… I was pretty sure my poems would meet with some applause, but at the worst, the roar of the Atlantic would drown the voice of censure, and the novelty of the Indian scenes make me forget neglect… My vanity was lighly gratified by the reception I got from the general publick, besides pocketing, all expenses deducted, near 20 pounds.

This was a decent sum, and his mention of it proves, that like all real writers, he wrote for money. The irony was that, had he stayed in Ayrshire, his landlord, Gavin Hamilton, was sure Burns could have sold another thousand copies had Wilson the printers rushed another printing through the presses, but Burns himself had other plans. He had only put out the first edition because he needed the money to emigrate, and the first thing he did with his book money was to pay nine guineas to James Brown, Insurance Broker, at Glasgow for passage in the brigantine the *Nancy*, under Captain Andrew Smith, berthed at Greenock, waiting to sail for the island of Antigua in Jamaica on or about 10 August.

The prospect obsessed him at this time. It was part of his wild, unconsidered Scottish escape plan that would free him from barren fields and fertile women, and let him do or die under the exotic West Indian sun. He wanted to forget everything and this was a congenial oblivion. Or so he thought. It was the kind of life decision only a poet could make, and he was stuck with it, despite the success of the Kilmarnock Edition. Fortunately, two friends of his patron, Dr Douglas, a man and wife, had already travelled in Jamaica overland between Savannah and Port Antonio, where Burns was due to take up work, and warned him that to do that journey in the worst season would expose him to the risk of pleuritic fever in that climate and he would do better to wait and take the *Bell* under Captain John Cathcart which was going direct to Kingston from Greenock in September. So Burns heeded their advice, especially as the master, Captain Cathcart, was a good

friend of Gavin Hamilton's, so the *Nancy* sailed with-
out him.

This delay allowed him to hear from Dr Blacklock
in Edinburgh who suggested he should try for his
second edition in Edinburgh. Edinburgh? It was
almost as foreign to him as Jamaica. Why not? He had
nothing to lose. So he let the second ship sail west
without him, and, hiring a pony, he set off at dawn one
November morning for the capital of Scotland.
Nonetheless, he was keeping his options open and
booked his third passage across the Atlantic Ocean.
This time, it was on the *Roselle* under Captain Hogg.
He used what was left of his book money to pay William
Sibbald and Company of Leith, where the *Roselle* waited
to sail for the Windward Islands on 10 November. This
time he hoped he might be third time lucky as an
emigrant. Meantime, Lord Glencairn, yet another
Mason, took him in hand and suddenly, every door in
Edinburgh, including that of William Creech, the
publisher, was opened to him. In no time, he was as
popular in the gentry's with-drawing rooms as the
performing pig in the Grassmarket, and recited for his
supper at the best tables in Edinburgh. But he wrote
nothing new in the capital except 'To A Haggis' and a
sweet little song, 'A Rosebud by my Early Walk', for a
12-year old girl. He hated his life among the literati
and he hated himself for pandering to them. He knew
he must get away or he'd never be his own man again.
The matter was decided for him when Jean Armour
was thrown into the Mauchilne street by her parents,

he did the honorable thing and married her. Once again, Poet Burns, now publicly proclaimed Bard of All Scotland, missed the boat.

Sadly, this tale of three ships did not allow him to embrace full-time 'quill-driving' as he called it; which was all he had ever wanted. Instead, he waved Clarinda off to her husband in Jamaica and he settled in Dumfries into the morass of domestic responsibilities and the brain-numbing, debilitating routine of a day job with the Customs and Excise. In one final, defiant burst of poetic genius he produced 'Tam o' Shanter' but, for the most part he gave himself over to the writing and rewriting of songs and the making of nine children, of whom only three survived to become dull adults. The Robert Burns Story ended in a whimper over an unpaid bill, his 37-year-old body ruined by a harsh, deprived boyhood and an excessive fame in early manhood. They gave him a splendid, military funeral which was inapt as it was tasteless.

The common people cried for him that day as the ruling classes turned away, leaving him as they thought to the anonymity of a pauper's grave but they reckoned without Scotland's love for this peasant polymath, a self-tutored autodidact of lyric genius, who was appreciated as a maker of songs but was and is still loved as a man. That's what makes him a hero, but of the Scottish kind, where his courage is not because of who he was, but despite who he was.

He has left us a book as a wee minding, and it is with

great Scottish pride and joy, I now invite you, the reader, to board THE KILMARNOCK EDITION, now so splendidly re-fitted by Luath Press as further evidence of his author-ship, and set sail in it with our hero on his timeless voyage to Parnassus.

And may he wave us off from the shore with his own words:

> No doubt I shall have much to answer for, yet my philosophy was simple enough; whatever mitigates the woes or increases the happiness of others, that is my criterion of goodness; what injures society as a whole, or any one person in it, that is my measure of iniquity.

Everything that is in this book is contained in these five lines, but please read on...

Dr John Cairney
2009

THE
TWA DOGS,
A TALE

'TWAS in that place o' Scotland's isle,
   That bears the name o' auld king
COIL,
Upon a bonie day in June,
When wearing thro' the afternoon,
Twa Dogs, that were na thrang at hame,
Forgather'd ance upon a time.

   The firſt I'll name, they ca'd him *Cæsar*,
Was keepet for His Honor's pleasure;
His hair, his size, his mouth, his lugs,
Shew'd he was nane o' Scotland's dogs,
But whalpet some place far abroad,
Where sailors gang to fish for Cod.

   His locked, letter'd, braw brass-collar
Shew'd him the *gentleman* an' *scholar*;
But tho' he was o' high degree,
The fient a pride na pride had he,
But wad hae spent an hour caressan,
Ev'n wi' a Tinkler-gipsey's *messan*:

At Kirk or Market, Mill or Smiddie,
Nae tawted *tyke*, tho' e'er sae duddie,
But he wad ſtan't, as glad to see him,
An' ſtroan't on ſtanes an' hillocks wi' him.

The tither was a *ploughman's collie*,
A rhyming, ranting, raving billie,
Wha for his friend an' comrade had him,
And in his freaks had *Luath* ca'd him,
After some dog in * *Highland sang*,
Was made lang syne, lord knows how lang.

He was a gash an' faithfu' *tyke*,
As ever lap a sheugh or dyke.
His honeſt, sonsie, baws'nt face,
Ay gat him friends in ilka place;
His breaſt was white, his towzie back,
Weel clad wi' coat o' glossy black;
His gawsie tail, wi' upward curl,
Hung owre his hurdies wi' a swirl.

* Cuchullin's dog in Ossian's Fingal.

Nae doubt but they were fain o' ither,
An' unco pack an' thick thegĵther;
Wi' social nose whyles snuff'd an' snowket;
Whyles mice and modewurks they howket;
Whyles scour'd awa in lang excursion,
An' worry'd ither in diversion;
Till tir'd at laſt wi' mony a farce,
They set them down upon their arse,
An' there began a lang digression
About the *lords o' the creation*.

CÆSAR

I've aften wonder'd, honeſt *Luath*,
What sort o' life poor dogs like you have;
An' when the *gentry's* life I saw,
What way *poor bodies* liv'd ava.

Our *Laird* gets in his racked rents,
His coals, his kane, an' a' his ſtents:
He rises when he likes himsel;
His flunkies answer at the bell;
He ca's his coach; he ca's his horse;
He draws a bonie, silken purse
As lang's my tail, whare thro' the ſteeks,
The yellow letter'd *Geordie* keeks.

Frae morn to een ît's nought but toiling,
At baking, roaſting, frying, boiling;
An' tho' the gentry firſt are ſteghan,
Yet ev'n the *ha' folk* fill their peghan
Wi' sauce, ragouts, an' sic like trashtrie,
That's lîttle short o' downright waſtrie.
Our *Whipper-in*, wee, blaſtet wonner,
Poor, worthless elf, ît eats a dinner,
Better than ony *Tenant-man*
His Honor has in a' the lan':
An' what poor *Cot-folk* pît their painch in,
I own ît's paſt my comprehension.

LUATH

Trowth, Cæsar, whyles their fash't enough;
A *Cotter* howkan in a sheugh,
Wi' dirty ſtanes biggan a dyke,
Bairan a quarry, an' sic like,
Himsel, a wife, he thus suſtains,
A smytrie o' wee, duddie weans,
An' nought but his han'-daurk, to keep
Them right an' tight in thack an' raep.

An' when they meet wi' sair disaſters,
Like loss o' health or want o' maſters,
Ye maiſt wad think, a wee touch langer,

An' they maun ſtarve o' cauld and hunger:
But how it comes, I never kent yet,
They're maiſtly wonderfu' contented;
An' buirdly chiels, and clever hizzies,
Are bred in sic a way as this is.

CÆSAR

But then, to see how ye're negleket,
How huff'd, an' cuff'd, an' disrespeket!
L—d man, our gentry care as little
For *delvers*, *ditchers*, an' sic cattle;
They gang as saucy by poor folk,
As I wad by a ſtinkan brock.

I've notic'd, on our Laird's *court-day*,
An' mony a time my heart's been wae,

Poor *tenant bodies*, scant o' cash,
How they maun thole a *factor's* snash;
He'll stamp an' threaten, curse an' swear,
He'll *apprehend* them, *poind* their gear;
While they maun stan', wi' aspect humble,
An' hear it a', an' fear an' tremble!

I see how folk live that hae riches;
But surely poor-folk maun be wretches!

LUATH

They're no sae wretched 's ane wad think;
Tho' constantly on poortith's brink,
They're sae accustom'd wi' the sight,
The view o't gies them little fright.

Then chance and fortune are sae guided,
They're ay in less or mair provided;
An' tho' fatigu'd wi' close employment,
A blink o' rest 's a sweet enjoyment.

The dearest comfort o' their lives,
Their grushie weans an' faithfu' wives;
The *prattling things* are just their pride,
That sweetens a' their fire side.

An' whyles twalpennie-worth o' *nappy*
Can mak the bodies unco happy;
They lay aside their private cares,
To mind the Kirk and State affairs;
They'll talk o' *patronage* an' *prieſts*,
Wi' kindling fury i' their breaſts,
Or tell what new taxation's comin,
An' ferlie at the folk in LON'ON.

As bleak-fac'd Hallowmass returns,
They get the jovial, rantan *Kirns*,
When *rural life*, of ev'ry ſtation,
Uniſte in common recreation;
Love blinks, Wiſt slaps, an' social Mirth
Forgets there's *care* upo' the earth.

That *merry day* the year begins,
They bar the door on froſty win's;
The nappy reeks wi' mantling ream,
An' sheds a heart-inspiring ſteam;
The luntan pipe, an' sneeshin mill,
Are handed round wi' right guid will;
The cantie, auld folks, crackan crouse,
The young anes rantan thro' the house—
My heart has been sae fain to see them,
That I for joy hae barket wi' them.

Still it's owre true that ye hae said,
Sic game is now owre aften play'd;
There's monie a creditable *stock*
O' decent, honest, fawsont folk,
Are riven out baith root an' branch,
Some rascal's pridefu' greed to quench,
Wha thinks to knit himsel the faster
In favor wi' some *gentle Master*,
Wha aiblins thrang a *parliamentin*,
For Britain's guid his saul indentin—

CÆSAR

Haith lad ye little ken about it;
For Britain's guid! guid faith! I doubt it.
Say rather, gaun as PREMIERS lead him,
An' saying *aye* or *no*'s they bid him:
At Operas an' Plays parading,
Mortgaging, gambling, masquerading:
Or maybe, in a frolic daft,
To HAGUE or CALAIS takes a waft,
To make a *tour* an' tak a whirl,
To learn *bon ton* an' see the worl'.

There, at VIENNA or VERSAILLES,
He rives his father's auld entails;
Or by MADRID he takes the rout,

To thrum *guittars* an' fecht wi' nowt;
Or down *Italian Vista* startles,
Wh—re-hunting amang groves o' myrtles:
Then bowses drumlie *German-water*,
To mak himsel look fair and fatter,
An' purge the bitter ga's an' cankers,
O' curst *Venetian* b—res an' ch—ncres.

For Britain's guid! for her destruction!
Wi' dissipation, feud an' faction!

LUATH

Hech man! dear sirs! is that the gate,
They waste sae mony a braw estate!
Are we sae foughten and harass'd
For gear to gang that gate at last!

O would they stay aback frae courts,
An' please themsels wi' countra sports,
It wad for ev'ry ane be better,
The *Laird*, the *Tenant*, an' the *Cotter!*
For thae frank, rantan, ramblan billies,
Fient haet o' them 's ill hearted fellows;
Except for breakin o' their timmer,
Or speakin lightly o' their *Limmer*,
Or shootin of a hare or moorcock,
The ne'er-a-bit they're ill to poor folk.

But will ye tell me, mafter *Cæsar*,
Sure *great folk's* life's a life o' pleasure?
Nae cauld nor hunger e'er can fteer them,
The vera thought o't need na fear them.

CÆSAR

L—d man, were ye but whyles where I am,
The *gentles* ye wad neer envy them!

It's true, they need na ftarve or sweat,
Thro' Winter's cauld, or Summer's heat;
They've nae fair-wark to craze their banes,
An' fill *auld-age* wi' grips an' granes;
But *human-bodies* are sic fools,
For a' their colledges an' schools,
That when nae *real* ills perplex them,
They *mak* enow themsels to vex them;
An' ay the less they hae to fturt them,
In like proportion, less will hurt them.

A country fellow at the pleugh,
His *acre's* till'd, he's right eneugh;
A country girl at her wheel,
Her *dizzen's* done, she's unco weel;
But Gentlemen, an' Ladies warft,

Wi' ev'n down *want o' wark* are curſt.
They loiter, lounging, lank an' lazy;
Tho' deil-haet ails them, yet uneasy;
Their days, insipid, dull an' taſteless,
Their nights, unquiet, lang an' reſtless.

An' ev'n their sports, their balls an' races,
Their galloping thro' public places,
There's sic parade, sic pomp an' art,
The joy can scarcely reach the heart.

The *Men* caſt out in *party-matches*,
Then sowther a' in deep debauches.
Ae night, they're mad wi' drink an' wh—ring,
Nieſt day their life is paſt enduring.

The *Ladies* arm-in-arm in cluſters,
As great an' gracious a' as siſters;
But hear their *absent thoughts* o' ither,
They're a run deils an' jads thegither.
Whyles, owre the wee bit cup an' platie,
They sip the *scandal-potion* pretty;
Or lee-lang nights, wi' crabbet leuks,
Pore owre the devil's *pictur'd beuks;*
Stake on a chance a farmer's ſtackyard,
An' cheat like ony *unhang'd blackguard*.

There's some exceptions, man an' woman;
But this is Gentry's life in common.

By this, the sun was out o' sight,
An' darker gloamin brought the night:
The *bum-clock* humm'd wi' lazy drone,
The kye stood rowtan i' the loan;
When up they gat an' shook their lugs,
Rejoic'd they were na *men* but *dogs*;
An' each took off his several way,
Resolv'd to meet some ither day.

SCOTCH DRINK

Gie him strong Drink *until he wink,*
  That's sinking in despair;
An' liquor *guid to fire his bluid,*
  That's prest wi' grief an' care:
There let him bowse an' deep carouse,
  Wi' bumpers flowing o'er,
Till he forgets his loves *or* debts,
  An' minds his griefs no more.

SOLOMON'S PROVERBS, xxxi 6, 7

L ET other Poets raise a fracas
  'Bout vines, an' wines, an' druken
    Bacchus,
An' crabbed names an' stories wrack us,
    An' grate our lug,
I sing the juice *Scotch bear* can mak us,
    In glass or jug.

  O thou, my MUSE! guid, auld
    SCOTCH DRINK!
Whether thro' wimplin worms thou jink,
Or, richly brown, ream owre the brink,

In glorious faem,
Inspire me, till I *lisp* an' *wink*,
To sing thy name!

Let husky Wheat the haughs adorn,
And Aîts set up their awnie horn,
An' Pease an' Beans, at een or morn,
Perfume the plain,
Leeze me on thee *John Barleycorn,*
Thou king o' grain!

On thee aft Scotland chows her cood,
In souple scones, the wale o' food!
Or tumbling in the boiling flood
Wi' kail an' beef;
But when thou pours thy ſtrong *heart's blood,*
There thou shines chief.

Food fills the wame, an' keeps us livin;
Tho' life's a gift no worth receivin,
When heavy-dragg'd wi' pine an' grievin;
But oil'd by thee,
The wheels o' life gae down-hill, scrievin,
Wi' rattlin glee.

Thou clears the head o' doîted Lear;
Thou chears the heart o' drooping Care;
Thou ſtrings the nerves o' Labor-sair,
      At's weary toil;
Thou ev'n brightens dark Despair,
      Wi' gloomy smile.

Aft, clad in massy, siller weed,
Wi' Gentles thou erects thy head;
Yet humbly kind, in time o' need,
      The *poor man's* wine;
His wee drap pirratch, or his bread,
      Thou kîtchens fine.

Thou art the life o' public haunts;
But thee, what were our fairs and rants?
Ev'n godly meetings o' the saunts,
      By thee inspir'd,
When gaping they besiege the *tents*,
      Are doubly fir'd.

That *merry night* we get the corn in,
O sweetly, then, thou reams the horn in!
Or reekan on a *New-year-mornin*
      In cog or bicker,
An' juſt a wee drap *sp'rîtual burn* in,
      An' guſty sucker!

When Vulcan gies his bellys breath,
An' Ploughmen gather wi' their graîth,
O rare! to see thee fizz an' freath
    I' the lugget caup!
Then *Burnewin* comes on like Death
    At ev'ry chap.

Nae mercy, then, for airn or ſteel;
The brawnie, banie, ploughman-chiel
Brings hard owrehip, wi' ſturdy wheel,
    The ſtrong forehammer,
Till block an' ſtuddie ring an' reel
    Wi' dinsome clamour.

When skirlin weanies see the light,
Thou maks the gossips clatter bright,
How fumbling coofs their dearies slight,
    Wae worth them for't!
While healths gae round to him wha, *tight*,
    Gies famous sport.

When neebors anger at a plea,
An' juſt as wud as wud can be,
How easy can the *barley-brie*
    Cement the quarrel!
It's aye the cheapeſt Lawyer's fee
    To taſte the barrel.

Alake! that e'er my *Muse* has reason,
To wyte her countrymen wi' treason!
But monie daily weet their weason
   Wi' liquors nice,
An' hardly, in a winter season,
   E'er spier her price.

 Wae worth that *Brandy*, burnan trash!
Fell source o' monie a pain an' brash!
Twins monie a poor, doylt, druken hash
   O' half his days;
An' sends, beside, auld *Scotland's* cash
   To her warst faes.

 Ye Scots wha wish auld Scotland well,
Ye chief, to you my tale I tell,
Poor, plackless devils like *mysel*,
   It sets you ill,
Wi' bitter, dearthfu' *wines* to mell,
   Or foreign gill.

 May *Gravels* round his blather wrench,
An' *Gouts* torment him, inch by inch,
Wha twists his gruntle wi' a glunch
   O' sour disdain,
Out owre a glass o' *Whisky-punch*
   Wi' honest men!

O *Whisky*! soul o' plays an' pranks!
Accept a *Bardie's* gratefu' thanks!
When wanting thee, what tuneless cranks
  Are my poor Verses!
Thou comes—they rattle i' their ranks
  At ither's arses!

Thee *Ferintosh!* O sadly loſt!
Scotland lament frae coaſt to coaſt!
Now colic-grips, an' barkin hoaſt,
  May kill us a';
For loyal Forbes' *Charter'd boaſt*
  Is ta'en awa!

Thae curſt horse-leeches o' th' Excise,
Wha mak the *Whisky ſtells* their prize!
Haud up thy han' *Deil*! ance, twice, *thrice!*
  There, sieze the blinkers!
An' bake them up in brunſtane pies
  For poor d—n'd *Drinkers.*

Fortune, if thou'll but gie me ſtill
Hale breeks, a scone, an' *whisky gill*,
An' rowth o' *rhyme* to rave at will,
  Tak a' the reſt,
An' deal't about as thy blind skill
  Directs thee beſt.

THE AUTHOR'S EARNEST CRY AND PRAYER, TO THE RIGHT HONORABLE AND HONORABLE, THE SCOTCH REPRESENTATIVES IN THE HOUSE OF COMMONS

Dearest of Distillation! last and best! —
— How art thou lost! —

PARODY ON MILTON

YE *Irish lords*, ye *knights an' squires*,
    Wha *represent* our *Brughs* an' *Shires*,
An' dousely manage our affairs
      In *Parliament*,
To you a simple Bardie's pray'rs
      Are humbly sent.

  Alas! my roupet *Muse* is haerse!
Your Honor's hearts wi' grief 'twad pierce,
To see her sittan on her arse
      Low i' the dust,
An' scriechan out prosaic verse,
      An' like to brust!

Tell them wha hae the chief direction,
Scotland an' *me's* in great affliction,
E'er sin' they laid that curſt reſtriction
      On AQUAVITÆ;
An' rouse them up to ſtrong conviction,
      An' move their pîty.

Stand forth and tell yon PREMIER YOUTH,
The honeſt, open, naked truth:
Tell him o' mine an' Scotland's drouth,
      His servants humble:
The muckle devil blaw you south,
      If ye dissemble!

Does ony *great man* glunch an' gloom?
Speak out an' never fash your thumb,
Let *poſts* an' *pensions* sink or swoom
      Wi' them wha grant them:
If honeſtly they canna come,
      Far better want them.

In gath'rin votes you were na slack,
Now ſtand as tightly by your tack:
Ne'er claw your lug, an' fidge your back,
      An' hum an' haw,
But raise your arm, an' tell your crack
      Before them a'.

Paint Scotland greetan owre her thrissle;
Her *mutchkin ſtowp* as toom's a whissle;
An' d—mn'd Excise-men in a bussle,
   Seizan a *Stell*,
Triumphant crushan't like a muscle
   Or laimpet shell.

Then on the tîther hand present her,
A blackguard *Smuggler*, right behint her,
An' cheek-for-chow, a chuffie *Vintner*,
   Colleaguing join,
Picking her pouch as bare as Winter,
   Of a' kind coin.

Is there, that bears the name o' SCOT,
But feels his heart's bluid rising hot,
To see his poor, auld Mîther's *pot*,
   Thus dung in ſtaves,
An' plunder'd o' her hindmoſt groat,
   By gallows knaves?

Alas! I'm but a nameless wight,
Trode i' the mire out o' sight!
But could I like MONTGOMERIES fight,
   Or gab like BOSWELL,
There's some *sark-necks* I wad *draw* tight,
   An' *tye* some *hose* well.

God bless your Honors, can ye see't,
The kind, auld, cantie Carlin greet,
An' no get warmly to your feet,
  An' gar them hear ît,
An' tell them, wi' a patriot-heat,
  Ye winna bear ît?

Some o' you nicely ken the laws,
To round the period an' pause,
An' wîth rhetoric clause on clause
  To mak harangues;
Then echo thro' Saint Stephen's wa's
  Auld Scotland's wrangs.

Dempster, a true-blue Scot I'se warran;
Thee, aîth-detesting, chaste *Kilkerran*;
An' that glib-gabbet Highland Baron,
  The Laird o' *Graham*;
And ane, a chap that's d—mn'd auldfarran,
  Dundas his name.

Erskine, a spunkie norland billie;
True Campbells, *Frederick* an' *Ilay*;
An' Livistone, the bauld *Sir Willie*;
  An' monie îthers,
Whom auld Demosthenes or Tully
  Might own for brîthers.

Arouse my boys! exert your mettle,
To get auld Scotland back her *kettle!*
Or faith! I'll wad my new pleugh-pettle,
   Ye'll see't or lang,
She'll teach you, wi' a reekan whittle,
   Anither sang.

 This while she's been in crankous mood,
Her *lost Militia* fir'd her bluid;
(Deil na they never mair do guid,
   Play'd her that pliskie!)
An' now she's like to rin red-wud
   About her *Whisky*.

 An' L—d! if ance they pit her till't,
Her tartan petticoat she'll kilt,
An' durk an' pistol at her belt,
   She'll tak the streets,
An' rin her whittle to the hilt,
   I' th' first the meets!

 For G—d-sake, Sirs! then speak her fair,
An' straik her cannie wi' the hair,
An' to the *muckle house* repair,
   Wi' instant speed,
An' strive, wi' a' your Wit an' Lear,
   To get remead.

Yon ill-tongu'd tinkler, *Charlie Fox*,
May taunt you wi' his jeers an' mocks;
But gie him't het, my hearty cocks!
      E'en cowe the cadie!
An' send him to his dicing box,
      An' sportin lady.

   Tell yon guid bluid o' auld *Boconnock's*,
I'll be his debt twa mashlum bonnocks,
An' drink his health in auld * *Nanse Tinnock's*
      Nine times a week,
If he some scheme, like tea an' winnocks,
      Wad kindly seek.

   Could he some *commutation* broach,
I'll pledge my aith in guid braid Scotch,
He need na fear their foul reproach
      Nor erudition,
Yon mixtie-maxtie, queer hotch-potch,
      The *Coalition*.

---

* A worthy old Hostess of the Author's in *Mauchline*,
  where he sometimes studies Politics over a glass of guid,
  auld *Scotch Drink*.

Auld Scotland has a raucle tongue;
She's just a devil wi' a rung;
An' if she promise auld or young
    To tak their part,
Tho' by the neck she should be strung,
    She'll no desert.

And now, ye chosen FIVE AND FORTY,
May still your Mither's heart support ye;
Then, tho' a *Minister* grow dorty,
    An' kick your place,
Ye'll snap your fingers, poor an' hearty,
    Before his face.

God bless your Honors, a' your days,
Wi' sowps o' kail and brats o' claise,
In spite o' a' the thievish kaes
    That haunt *St. Jamie's!*
Your humble Bardie sings an' prays
    While *Rab* his name is.

POSTSCRIPT

Let half-starv'd slaves in warmer skies,
See future wines, rich-clust'ring, rise;
Their lot auld Scotland ne'er envies,
But blythe an' frisky,
She eyes her freeborn, martial boys,
Tak aff their Whisky.

What tho' their Phœbus kinder warms,
While Fragrance blooms an' Beauty charms!
When wretches range, in famish'd swarms,
The scented groves,
Or hounded forth, *dishonor* arms
In hungry droves.

Their *gun's* a burden on their shouther;
They downa bide the stink o' *powther*;
Their bauldest thought's a hank'ring swither,
To stan' or rin,
Till skelp — a shot— they're aff, a' throw'ther,
To save their skin.

But bring a SCOTCHMAN frae his hill,
Clap in his cheek a *Highland gill*,
Say, such is royal GEORGE'S will,
  An' there's the foe,
He has ne thought but how to kill
  Twa at a blow.

Nae cauld, faint-hearted doubtings tease him;
Death comes, wi' fearless eye he sees him;
Wi' bluidy han' a welcome gies him;
  An' when he fa's,
His lateſt draught o' breathin lea'es him
  In faint huzzas.

Sages their solemn een may ſteek,
An' raise a philosophic reek,
An' physically causes seek,
  In *clime* an' *season*,
But tell me *Whisky's* name in Greek,
  I'll tell the reason.

SCOTLAND, my auld, respected Mîther!
Tho' whyles ye moiſtify your leather,
Till whare ye sît, on craps o' heather,
  Ye tine your dam;
FREEDOM and WHISKY gang the-gîther,
  Tak aff your *dram*!

THE

HOLY FAIR

A robe of seeming truth and truſt
  Hid crafty observation;
And secret hung, with poison'd cruſt,
  The dirk of Defamation:
A mask that like the gorget show'd,
  Dye-varying, on the pigeon;
And for a mantle large and broad,
  He wrapt him in Religion.

HYPOCRISY A-LA-MODE

I

UPON a simmer Sunday morn,
  When Nature's face is fair,
I walked forth to view the corn,
  An' snuff the callor air.
The rising sun, our GALSTON Muirs,
  Wi' glorious light was glintan;
The hares were hirplan down the furrs,
  The lav'rocks they were chantan
    Fu' sweet that day.

II

As lightsomely I glowr'd abroad,
    To see a scene sae gay,
Three *hizzies*, early at the road,
    Cam skelpan up the way.
Twa had manteeles o' dolefu' black,
    But ane wi' lyart lining;
The third, that gaed a wee a-back,
    Was in the fashion shining
        Fu' gay that day.

III

The *twa* appear'd like sisters twin,
    In feature, form an' claes;
Their visage wither'd, lang an' thin,
    An' sour as ony slaes:
The *third* cam up, hap-step-an'-loup,
    As light as ony lambie,
An' wi' a curchie low did stoop,
    As soon as e'er she saw me,
        Fu' kind that day.

IV

Wi' bonnet aff, quoth I, 'Sweet lass,
   'I think ye seem to ken me;
'I'm sure I've seen that bonie face,
   'But yet I canna name ye.'
Quo' she, an' laughan as she spak,
   An' taks me by the han's,
'Ye, for my sake, hae gien the feck
   'Of a' the *ten comman's*
       A screed some day.'

V

'My name is FUN — your cronie dear,
   'The neareſt friend ye hae;
'An' this is SUPERSTITION here,
   'An' that's HYPOCRISY.
'I'm gaun to ********* *holy fair*,
   'To spend an hour in daffin:
'Gin ye'll go there, you runkl'd pair,
   'We will get famous laughin
       At them this day.'

VI

Quoth I, 'Wîth a' my heart, I'll do't;
　'I'll get my sunday's sark on,
'An' meet you on the holy spot;
　'Faîth, we'se hae fine remarkin!'
Then I gaed hame at crowdie-time,
　An' soon I made me ready;
For roads were clad, frae side to side,
　Wi' monie a wearie body,
　　　　In droves that day.

VII

Here, farmers gash, in ridin graîth,
　Gaed hoddan by their cotters;
There, swankies young, in braw braid-claîth,
　Are springan owre the gutters.
The lasses, skelpan barefît, thrang,
　In silks an' scarlets glîtter;
Wi' *sweet-milk cheese*, in monie a whang,
　An' *farls*, bak'd wi' butter,
　　　　Fu' crump that day.

VIII

When by the *plate* we set our nose,
    Weel heaped up wi' ha'pence,
A greedy glowr *black-bonnet* throws,
    An' we maun draw our tippence.
Then in we go to see the show,
    On ev'ry side they're gath'ran;
Some carryan dails, some chairs an' ſtools,
    An' some are busy bleth'ran
        Right loud that day.

IX

Here ſtands a shed to fend the show'rs,
    An' screen our countra Gentry;
There, *racer Jess*, an' twathree wh—res,
    Are blinkan at the entry.
Here ſits a raw o' tittlan jads,
    Wi' heaving breaſts an' bare neck;
An' there, a batch o' *Wabſter lads*,
    Blackguarding frae K*******ck
        For *fun* this day.

X

Here, some are thinkan on their sins,
    An' some upo' their claes;
Ane curses feet that fyl'd his shins,
    Anither sighs an' prays:
On this hand sits an *Elect* swatch,
    Wi' screw'd-up, grace-proud faces;
On that, a set o' chaps, at watch,
    Thrang winkan on the lasses
        To *chairs* that day.

XI

O happy is that man, an' blest!
    Nae wonder that it pride him!
Whase ain dear lass, that he likes best,
    Comes clinkan down beside him!
Wi' arm repos'd on the *chair-back*,
    He sweetly does compose him;
Which, by degrees, flips round her *neck*,
    An's loof upon her *bosom*
        Unkend that day.

XII

Now a' the congregation o'er
   Is silent expectation;
For ****** speels the holy door,
   Wi' tidings o' s—lv—t—n.
Should *Hornie*, as in ancient days,
   'Mang sons o' G— present him,
The vera sight o' ******'s face,
   To's ain *het hame* had sent him
      Wi' fright that day.

XIII

Hear how he clears the points o' Faith
   Wi' rattlin an' thumpin!
Now meekly calm, now wild in wrath,
   He's stampan, an' he's jumpan!
His lengthen'd chin, his turn'd up snout
   His eldritch squeel an' gestures,
O how they fire the heart devout,
   Like *cantharidian* plaisters
      On sic a day!

XIV

But hark! the *tent* has chang'd ît's voice;
 There's peace an' reſt nae langer;
For a' the *real judges* rise,
 They canna sît for anger.
***** opens out his cauld harangues,
 On *practice* and on *morals*;
An' aff the *godly* pour in thrangs,
 To gie the jars an' barrels
   A lift that day.

XV

What signifies his barren shine,
 Of *moral pow'rs* an' *reason*?
His English ſtyle, an' geſture fine,
 Are a' clean out o' season
Like SOCRATES or ANTONINE,
 Or some auld pagan heathen,
The *moral man* he does define,
 But ne'er a word o' *faîth* in
   That's right that day.

XVI

In guid time comes an antidote
   Against sic poosion'd nostrum;
For *******, frae the water-fit
   Ascends the *holy rostrum*:
See, up he's got the word o' G—,
   An' meek an' mim has view'd it,
While COMMON-SENSE has taen the road,
   An' aff, an' up the *Cowgate*
      Fast, fast that day.

XVII

Wee ****** niest, the Guard relieves,
   An' Orthodoxy raibles,
Tho' in his heart he weel believes.
   An' thinks it auld wives' fables:
But faith! the birkie wants a *Manse*,
   So, cannilie he hums them;
Altho' his *carnal* Wit an' Sense
   Like hafflins-wise o'ercomes him
      At times that day.

XVIII

Now, butt an' ben, the Change-house fills,
    Wi' *yill-caup* Commentators:
Here's crying out for bakes an' gills,
    An' there the pint-ſtowp clatters;
While thick an' thrang, an' loud an' lang,
    Wi' *Logic*, an' wi' *Scripture*,
They raise a din, that, in the end,
    Is like to breed a rupture
            O' wrath that day.

XIX

Leeze me on Drink! ît gies us mair
    Than eîther School or Colledge:
It kindles Wît, ît waukens Lear,
    It pangs us fou o' Knowledge.
Be't *whisky-gill* or *penny-wheep*,
    Or ony ſtronger potion,
It never fails, on drinkin deep,
    To kîttle up our *notion*,
            By night or day.

XX

The lads an' lasses, blythely bent
　　To mind baîth *saul* an' *body*,
Sît round the table, weel content,
　　An' ſteer about the *toddy*.
On this ane's dress, an' that ane's leuk,
　　They're makin observations;
While some are cozie i' the neuk,
　　An' forming *assignations*
　　　　To meet some day.

XXI

But now the L—'s ain trumpet touts,
　　Till a' the hills are rairan,
An' echos back return the shouts;
　　Black ****** is na spairan:
His piercin words, like Highlan swords,
　　Divide the joints an' marrow;
His talk o' H—ll, whare devils dwell,
　　Our vera * 'Sauls does harrow'
　　　　Wi' fright that day!

* Shakespeare's Hamlet.

XXII

A vast, unbottom'd, boundless *Pit*,
    Fill'd fou o' *lowan brunstane*,
Whase raging flame, an' scorching heat,
    Wad melt the hardest whun-stane!
The *half asleep* start up wi' fear,
    An' think they hear it roaran,
When presently it does appear,
    'Twas but some neebor *snoran*
        Asleep that day.

XXIII

'Twad be owre lang a tale to tell,
    How monie stories past,
An' how they crouded to the yill,
    When they were a' dismist:
How drink gaed round, in cogs an' caups,
    Amang the furms an' benches;
An' *cheese* an' *bread*, frae women's laps,
    Was dealt about in lunches,
        An' dawds that day.

XXIV

In comes a gawsie, gash *Guidwife*,
   An' sits down by the fire,
Syne draws her *kebbuck* an' her knife;
   The lasses they are shyer.
The auld *Guidmen*, about the *grace,*
   Frae side to side they bother,
Till some ane by his bonnet lays,
   An' gies them't, like a tether,
      Fu' lang that day.

XXV

Waesucks! for him that gets nae lass,
   Or lasses that hae naething!
Sma' need has he to say a grace,
   Or melvie his braw claithing!
O *Wives* be mindfu', ance yoursel,
   How bonie lads ye wanted,
An' dinna, for a *kebbuck-heel*,
   Let lasses be affronted
      On sic a day!

XXVI

Now *Clinkumbell*, wi' rattlan tow,
　　Begins to jow an' croon;
Some swagger hame, the beſt they dow,
　　Some waĭt the afternoon.
At slaps the billies halt a blink,
　　Till lasses ſtrip their shoon:
Wi' *faĭth* an' *hope*, an' *love* an' *drink*,
　　They're a' in famous tune
　　　　　For crack that day.

XXVII

How monie hearts this day converts,
　　O' sinners and o' Lasses!
Their hearts o' ſtane, gin night are gane,
　　As saft as ony flesh is.
There's some are fou o' *love divine*;
　　There's some are fou o' *brandy*;
An' monie jobs that day begin,
　　May end in *Houghmagandie*
　　　　　Some ĭther day.

ADDRESS TO THE DEIL

O Prince, O chief of many throned pow'rs,
That led th' embattl'd Seraphim to war—

Milton

O THOU, whatever title suit thee!
    Auld Hornie, Satan, Nick, or Clootie,
Wha in yon cavern grim an' sootie,
        Clos'd under hatches,
Spairges about the brunstane cootie,
        To scaud poor wretches!

    Hear me, *auld Hangie,* for a wee,
An' let poor, *damned bodies* bee;
I'm sure sma' pleasure it can gie,
        Ev'n to a *deil,*
To skelp an' scaud poor dogs like me,
        An' hear us squeel!

    Great is thy pow'r, an' great thy fame;
Far kend an' noted is thy name;
An' tho' yon *lowan heugh's* thy hame,
        Thou travels far;
An' faith! thou's neither lag nor lame;
        Nor blate nor scaur.

Whyles, ranging like a roaran lion,
For prey, a' holes an' corners tryin;
Whyles, on the strong-wing'd Tempest flyin,
  Tirlan the *kirks*;
Whyles, in the human bosom pryin,
  Unseen thou lurks.

I've heard my rev'rend *Graunie* say,
In lanely glens ye like to stray;
Or where auld, ruin'd castles, gray
  Nod to the moon,
Ye fright the nightly wand'rer's way,
  Wi' eldritch croon.

When twilight did my *Graunie* summon,
To say her pray'rs, douse, honest woman!
Aft 'yont the dyke she's heard you bumman,
  Wi' eerie drone;
Or, rustling, thro' the boortries coman,
  Wi' heavy groan.

Ae dreary, windy, winter night,
The stars shot down wi' sklentan light,
Wi' you, *mysel*, I gat a fright,
  Ayont the lough;
Ye, like a *rash-buss*, stood in sight,
  Wi' waving sugh.

The cudgel in my nieve did shake,
Each briſtl'd hair ſtood like a ſtake,
When wi' an eldritch, ſtoor *quaick*, *quaick*,
      Amang the springs,
Awa ye squatter'd like a *drake*,
        On whiſtling wings.

Let *Warlocks* grim, an' wither'd *Hags*,
Tell how wi' you on ragweed nags,
They skim the muirs an' dizzy crags,
      Wi' wicked speed;
And in kirk-yards renew their leagues,
        Owre howcket dead.

Thence, countra wives, wi' toil an' pain,
May plunge an' plunge the *kirn* in vain;
For Oh! the yellow treasure's taen
      By witching skill;
An' dawtet, twal-pint *Hawkie's* gane
        As yell's the Bill.

Thence, myſtic knots mak great abuse,
On *Young-Guidmen*, fond, keen an' croose;
When the beſt *wark-lume* i' the house,
      By cantraip wit,
Is inſtant made no worth a louse,
        Juſt at the bit.

When thowes dissolve the snawy hoord,
An' float the jinglan icy boord,
Then, *Water-kelpies* haunt the foord,
    By your direction,
An' nighted Trav'llers are allur'd
    To their deſtruction.

An' aft your moss-traversing *Spunkies*
Decoy the wight that late an' drunk is:
The bleezan, curſt, mischievous monkies
    Delude his eyes,
Till in some miry slough he sunk is,
    Ne'er mair to rise.

When MASONS' myſtic *word* an' *grip*,
In ſtorms an' tempeſts raise you up,
Some cock or cat, your rage maun ſtop,
    Or, ſtrange to tell!
The *youngeſt Brother* ye wad whip
    Aff ſtraught to *H—ll*.

Lang syne in EDEN'S bonie yard,
When youthfu' lovers firſt were pair'd,
An' all the Soul of Love they shar'd,
    The raptur'd hour,
Sweet on the fragrant, flow'ry swaird,
    In shady bow'r.

Then you, ye auld, snick-drawing dog!
Ye cam to Paradise incog,
An' play'd on man a cursed brogue,
  (Black be your fa'!)
An' gied the infant warld a shog,
  'Maiſt ruin'd a'.

D'ye mind that day, when in a bizz,
Wi' reeket duds, an' reeſtet gizz,
Ye did present your smoutie phiz,
  'Mang better folk,
An' sklented on the *man of Uzz*,
  Your spîtefu' joke?

An how ye gat him i' your thrall,
An' brak him out o' house an' hal',
While scabs an' botches did him gall,
  Wi' bîtter claw,
An' lows'd his ill-tongu'd, wicked *Scawl*
  Was warſt ava?

But a' your doings to rehearse,
Your wily snares an' fechtin fierce,
Sin' that day * MICHAEL did you pierce,
  Down to this time,

* Vide Milton, Book 6th.

Wad ding a' *Lallan* tongue, or *Erse*,
   In Prose or Rhyme.

 An' now, auld *Cloots*, I ken ye're thinkan,
A certain *Bardie's* rantin, drinkin,
Some luckless hour will send him linkan,
   To your black pît;
But faîth! he'll turn a corner jinkan,
   An' cheat you yet.

 But fare-you-weel, auld *Nickie-ben*!
O wad ye tak a thought an' men'!
Ye aiblins might — I dinna ken —
   Still hae a *stake* —
I'm wae to think upo' yon den,
   Ev'n for your sake!

THE DEATH AND DYING WORDS OF POOR MAILIE,

THE AUTHOR'S ONLY PET YOWE,

AN UNCO MOURNFU' TALE

AS MAILIE, an' her lambs thegither,
   Was ae day nibbling on the tether,
Upon her cloot she coost a hitch,
An' owre she warsl'd in the ditch:
There, groaning, dying, she did ly,
When * *Hughoc* he cam doytan by.

   Wi' glowrin een, an' lifted han's,
Poor *Hughoc* like a statue stan's;
He saw her days were near hand ended,
But, waes my heart! he could na mend it!
He gaped wide, but naething spak,
At length poor *Mailie* silence brak.

   'O thou, whase lamentable face
Appears to mourn my woefu' case!
My *dying words* attentive hear,
An' bear them to my *Master* dear.

---

* A neibor herd-callan.

Tell him, if e'er again he keep
As muckle gear as buy a *sheep*,
O, bid him never tye them mair,
Wi' wicked ſtrings o' hemp or hair!
But ca' them out to park or hill,
An' let them wander at their will:
So, may his flock increase an' grow
To *scores* o' lambs, an' *packs* of woo'!

Tell him, he was a Maſter kin',
An' ay was guid to me an' mine;
An' now my *dying* charge I gie him,
My helpless *lambs*, I truſt them wi' him.

O, bid him save their harmless lives,
Frae dogs an' tods, an' butchers' knives!
But gie them guid *cow-milk* their fill,
Till they be fît to fend themsel;
An' tent them duely, e'en an' morn,
Wi' taets o' *hay* an' ripps o' *corn*.

An' may they never learn the gaets,
Of ither vile, wanreſtfu' *Pets!*
To slink thro' slaps, an' reave an' ſteal,
At ſtacks o' pease, or ſtocks o' kail.
So may they, like their great *forbears*,
For monie a year come thro' the sheers:
So *wives* will gie them bits o' bread,
An' *bairns* greet for them when they're dead.

My poor *toop-lamb*, my son an' heir,
O, bid him breed him up wi' care!
An' if he live to be a beaſt,
To pit some havins in his breaſt!
An' warn him ay at ridin time,
To ſtay content wi' *yowes* at hame;
An' no to rin an' wear his cloots,
Like ither menseless, graceless brutes.

An' nieſt my *yowie*, silly thing,
Gude keep thee frae a *tether ſtring!*
O, may thou ne'er forgather up,
Wi' onie blaſtet, moorlan *toop*;
But ay keep mind to moop an' mell,
Wi' sheep o' credit like thysel!

And now, *my bairns*, wi' my laſt breath,
I lea'e my blessin wi' you baîth:
An' when ye think upo' your Mîther,
Mind to be kind to ane anîther.

Now, honeſt Hughoc, dinna fail,
To tell my Maſter a' my tale;
An' bid him burn this cursed *tether*,
An' for thy pains thou'se get my blather.'

This said, poor *Mailie* turn'd her head,
An' clos'd her een amang the dead!

POOR MAILIE'S ELEGY

L AMENT in rhyme, lament in prose,
   Wi' saut tears trickling down your nose;
Our *Bardie's* fate is at a close,
      Past a' remead!
The last, sad cape-stane of his woes;
      Poor Mailie's dead!

It's no the loss o' warl's gear,
That could sae bitter draw the tear,
Or make our *Bardie*, dowie, wear
      The mourning weed:
He's lost a friend and neebor dear,
      In *Mailie* dead.

Thro' a' the town she trotted by him;
A lang half-mile she could descry him;
Wi' kindly bleat, when she did spy him,
      She ran wi' speed:
A friend mair faithfu' ne'er came nigh him,
      Than *Mailie* dead.

I wat she was a *sheep* o'sense,
An' could behave hersel wi' mense:
I'll say't, she never brak a fence,
   Thro' thievish greed.
Our *Bardie*, lanely, keeps the spence
   Sin' *Mailie's* dead.

Or, if he wanders up the howe,
Her living image in *her yowe*,
Comes bleating till him, owre the knowe,
   For bits o' bread;
An' down the briny pearls rowe
   For *Mailie* dead.

She was nae get o' moorlan tips,
Wi' tauted ket, an' hairy hips;
For her forbears were brought in ships,
   Frae 'yont the TWEED:
A bonier *fleesh* ne'er cross'd the clips
   Than *Mailie's* dead.

Wae worth that man wha first did shape,
That vile, wanchancie thing — *a raep!*
It maks guid fellows girn an' gape,
  Wi' chokin dread;
An' *Robin's* bonnet wave wi' crape
  For *Mailie* dead.

O, a' ye *Bards* on bonie DOON!
An' wha on AIRE your chanters tune!
Come, join the melancholious croon
  O' *Robin's* reed!
His heart will never get aboon!
  His *Mailie's* dead!

TO J . S ****

Friendship, mysterious cement of the soul!
Sweet'ner of Life, and solder of Society!
I owe thee much —

BLAIR

DEAR S****, the sleest, pawkie thief,
    That e'er attempted stealth or rief,
Ye surely hae some warlock-breef
    Owre human hearts;
For ne'er a bosom yet was prief
    Against your arts.

    For me, I swear by sun an' moon,
And ev'ry star that blinks aboon.
Ye've cost me twenty pair o' shoon
    Just gaun to see you;
And ev'ry ither pair that's done,
    Mair taen I'm wi' you.

    That auld, capricious carlin, *Nature,*
To mak amends for scrimpet stature,
She's turn'd you off, a human-creature
    On her *first* plan,
And in her freaks, on ev'ry feature,
    She's wrote, *the Man.*

Just now I've taen the fit o' rhyme,
My barmie noddle's working prime,
My fancy yerket up sublime
    Wi' hasty summon:
Hae ye a leisure-moment's time
    To hear what's comin?

Some rhyme a neebor's name to lash;
Some rhyme, (vain thought!) for needfu' cash;
Some rhyme to court the countra clash,
    An' raise a din;
For me, an *aim* I never fash;
    I rhyme for *fun.*

The star that rules my luckless lot,
Has fated me the russet coat,
An' damn'd my fortune to the groat;
    But, in requit,
Has blest me with a *random-shot*
    O' countra wit.

This while my notion's taen a sklent,
To try my fate in guid, black *prent*;
But still the mair I'm that way bent,
    Something cries, 'Hoolie!
'I red you, honest man, tak tent!
    Ye'll shaw your folly.

'There's ither Poets, much your betters,
'Far seen in *Greek*, deep men o' *letters*,
'Hae thought they had ensur'd their debtors,
          'A' future ages;
'Now moths deform in shapeless tatters,
          'Their unknown pages.'

          Then farewel hopes of Laurel-boughs,
To garland my poetic brows!
Henceforth, I'll rove where busy ploughs
          Are whistling thrang,
An' teach the lanely heights an' howes
          My rustic sang.

          I'll wander on with tentless heed,
How never-halting moments speed,
Till fate shall snap the brittle thread;
          Then, all unknown,
I'll lay me with th' *inglorious dead*,
          Forgot and gone!

          But why, o' Death, begin a tale?
Just now we're living sound an' hale;
Then top and maintop croud the sail,
          Heave *Care* o'er-side!
And large, before Enjoyment's gale,
          Let's tak the tide.

This life, sae far's I understand,
Is a' enchanted fairy-land,
Where Pleasure is the Magic-wand,
      That, wielded right,
Maks Hours like Minutes, hand in hand,
      Dance by fu' light.

The *magic-wand* then let us wield;
For, ance that five an' forty's speel'd,
See, crazy, weary, joyless Eild,
      Wi' wrinkl'd face,
Comes hostan, hirplan owre the field,
      Wi' creeping pace.

When ance *life's day* draws near the gloamin,
Then fareweel vacant, careless roamin;
An' fareweel chearfu' tankards foamin,
      An' social noise;
An' fareweel dear, deluding woman,
      The joy of joys!

O *Life*! how pleasant in thy morning,
Young Fancy's rays the hills adorning!
Cold-pausing Caution's lesson scorning,
      We frisk away,
Like school-boys, at th' expected warning,
      To joy and play.

We wander there, we wander here,
We eye the *rose* upon the brier,
Unmindful that the *thorn* is near,
  Among the leaves;
And tho' the puny wound appear,
  Short while it grieves.

Some, lucky, find a flow'ry spot,
For which they never toil'd nor swat;
They drink the *sweet* and eat the *fat*,
  But care or pain;
And hap'ly, eye the barren hut,
  With high disdain.

With steady aim, Some Fortune chase;
Keen hope does ev'ry sinew brace;
Thro' fair, thro' foul, they urge the race,
  And sieze the prey:
Then canie, in some cozie place,
  They close the *day*.

And others, like your humble servan',
Poor wights! nae rules nor roads observin;
To right or left, eternal swervin,
  They zig-zag on;
Till curst with Age, obscure an' starvin,
  They aften groan.

Alas! what bitter toil an' ſtraining —
But truce with peevish, poor complaining!
Is Fortune's fickle *Luna* waning?
      E'en let her gang!
Beneath what light she has remaining,
      Let's sing our Sang.

My pen I here fling to the door,
And kneel, 'Ye *Pow'rs*, and warm implore,
'Tho' I should wander *Terra* o'er,
      'In all her climes,
'Grant me but this, I ask no more,
      'Ay rowth o' rhymes.

'Gie dreeping roaſts to *countra Lairds*,
'Till icicles hing frae their beards;
'Gie fine braw claes to fine *Life-guards*,
      'And *Maids of Honor*;
'And yill an' whisky gie to *Cairds*,
      'Until they sconner.

'A *Title*, DEMPSTER merits it;
'A *Garter* gie to WILLIE PIT;
'Gie Wealth to some be-ledger'd Cit,
      'In cent per cent;
'But give me real, ſterling Wit,
      'And I'm content.

'While ye are pleas'd to keep me hale,
'I'll sît down o'er my scanty meal,
'Be't *water-brose*, or *muslin-kail*,
   'Wi' chearfu' face,
'As lang's the Muses dinna fail
   'To say the grace.'

An anxious e'e I never throws
Behint my lug, or by my nose;
I jouk beneath Misfortune's blows
   As weel's I may;
Sworn foe to *sorrow*, *care*, and *prose*,
   I rhyme away.

O ye, douse folk, that live by rule,
Grave, tideless-blooded, calm and cool,
Compar'd wi' you—O fool! fool! fool!
   How much unlike!
Your hearts are juſt a ſtanding pool,
   Your lives, a dyke!

Nae hare-brain'd, sentimental traces,
In your unletter'd, nameless faces!
In *arioso* trills and graces
   Ye never ſtray,
But *gravissimo*, solemn basses
   Ye hum away.

Ye are sae *grave*, nae doubt ye're *wise*;
Nae ferly tho' ye do despise
The hairum-scairum, ram-ſtam boys,
  The rambling squad:
I see ye upward caſt your eyes—
  —Ye ken the road—

  Whilſt I—but I shall haud me there—
Wi' you I'll scarce gang *ony where*—
Then *Jamie*, I shall say nae mair,
  But quat my sang,
Content *with* YOU to mak a *pair*,
  Whare'er I gang.

A
D R E A M

Thoughts, words and deeds, the Statute blames with reason;
But surely Dreams *were ne'er indicted Treason.*

ON READING, IN THE PUBLIC PAPERS, THE LAUREATE'S ODE,
WITH THE OTHER PARADE OF JUNE 4TH, 1786, THE AUTHOR
WAS NO SOONER DROPT ASLEEP, THAN HE IMAGINED
HIMSELF TRANSPORTED TO THE BIRTH-DAY LEVEE; AND, IN
HIS DREAMING FANCY, MADE THE FOLLOWING ADDRESS.

I

GUID-MORNIN to your MAJESTY!
　　May heaven augment your blisses,
On ev'ry new *Birth-day* ye see,
　　A humble Bardie wishes!
My Bardship here, at your Levee,
　　On sic a day as this is,
Is sure an uncouth sight to see,
　　Amang thae Birth-day dresses
　　　　Sae fine this day.

II

I see ye're complimented thrang,
    By many a *lord* an' *lady*;
'God save the King' 's a cukoo sang
    That's unco easy said ay:
The *Poets* too, a venal gang,
    Wi' rhymes weel-turn'd an' ready,
Wad gar you trow ye ne'er do wrang,
    But ay unerring steady,
            On sic a day.

III

For me! before a Monarch's face,
    Ev'n *there* I winna flatter;
For neither Pension, Post, nor Place,
    Am I your humble debtor:
So, nae reflection on YOUR GRACE,
    Your Kingship to bespatter;
There's monie *waur* been o' the Race,
    And aiblins *ane* been better
            Than You this day.

IV

'Tis very true, my sovereign King,
   My skill may weel be doubted;
But *Facts* are cheels that winna ding,
   An' downa be disputed:
Your *royal nest*, beneath *Your* wing,
   Is e'en right reft an' clouted,
And now the third part o' the string,
   An' less, will gang about it
      Than did ae day.

V

Far be't frae me that I aspire
   To blame your Legislation,
Or say, ye wisdom want, or fire,
   To rule this mighty nation;
But faith! I muckle doubt, my SIRE,
   Ye've trusted 'Ministration,
To chaps, wha, in a *barn* or *byre*,
   Wad better fill'd their station
      Than *courts* yon day.

VI

And now Ye've gien auld *Britain* peace,
  Her broken shins to plaister;
Your sair taxation does her fleece,
  Till she has scarce a tester:
For me, thank God, my life's a *lease*,
  Nae *bargain* wearing faster,
Or faith! I fear, that, wi' the geese,
  I shortly boost to pasture
        I' the craft some day.

VII

I'm no mistrusting *Willie Pit*,
  When taxes he enlarges,
(An' *Will's* a true guid fallow's get,
  A Name not Envy spairges)
That he intends to pay your *debt*,
  An' lessen a' your *charges*;
But, G—d-sake! let nae *saving-fit*
  Abridge your bonie *Barges*
        An' *Boats* this day.

VIII

Adieu, my LIEGE! may Freedom geck
   Beneath your high protection;
An' may Ye rax Corruption's neck,
   And gie her for dissection!
But since I'm here, I'll no neglect,
   In loyal, true affection,
To pay your QUEEN, with due respect,
   My fealty an' subjection
       This great Birth-day.

IX

Hail, *Majesty most Excellent!*
   While Nobles strive to please Ye,
Will Ye accept a Compliment,
   A simple Bardie gies Ye?
Thae bonie Bairntime, Heav'n has lent,
   Still higher may they heeze Ye
In bliss, till Fate some day is sent,
   For ever to release Ye
       Frae Care that day.

X

For you, young Potentate o' W—,
   I tell your *Highness* fairly,
Down Pleasure's stream, wi' swelling sails,
   I'm tauld ye're driving rarely;
But some day ye may gnaw your nails,
   An' curse your folly fairly,
That e'er ye brak Diana's *pales*,
   Or rattl'd dice wi' *Charlie*
       By night or day.

XI

Yet aft a ragged *Cowte's* been known,
   To mak a noble *Aiver*;
So, ye may dousely fill a Throne,
   For a' their clish-ma-claver:
There, Him at *Agincourt* wha shone
   Few better were or braver;
And yet, wi' funny, queer *Sir* * *John*,
   He was an unco shaver
       For monie a day.

* Sir John Falstaff, Vide Shakespeare.

XII

For you, right rev'rend O—,
　　Nane sets the *lawn-sleeve* sweeter,
Altho' a ribban at your lug
　　Wad been a dress compleater:
As ye disown yon paughty dog,
　　That *bears* the Keys of Peter,
Then swîth! An' get a *wife* to hug,
　　Or trouth! Ye'll ſtain the *Mître*
　　　　Some luckless day.

XIII

Young, royal TARRY-BREEKS, I learn,
　　Ye've lately come athwart her;
A glorious † *Galley*, ſtem and ſtern,
　　Weel rigg'd for *Venus barter*;
But firſt hang out that she'll discern
　　Your *hymeneal Charter*,
Then heave aboard your *grapple airn*,
　　An', large upon her *quarter*,
　　　　Come full that day.

† Alluding to the newspaper account of a certain
royal Sailor's Amour.

XIV

Ye laſtly, bonie blossoms a',
   Ye *royal Lasses* dainty,
Heav'n mak you guid as weel as braw,
   An' gie you *lads* a plenty:
But sneer na *Britiſh-boys* awa;
   For King's are unco scant ay,
An' German Gentles are but *sma'*,
   They're better juſt than *want ay*
      On onie day.

XV

God bless you a'! consider now,
   Ye're unco muckle dautet;
But ere the *course* o' life be through,
   It may be bitter sautet:
An' I hae seen their *coggie* fou,
   That yet hae tarrow't at it,
But or the *day* was done, I trow,
   The laggen they hae clautet
      Fu' clean that day.

THE
VISION
DUAN FIRST *

THE fun had clos'd the *winter-day*,
   The Curlers quat their roaring play,
And hunger'd Maukin taen her way
     To kail-yards green,
While faithless snaws ilk ſtep betray
     Whare she has been.

   The Thresher's weary *flingin-tree*,
The lee-lang day had tir'd me;
And when the Day had clos'd his e'e,
     Far i' the Weſt,
Ben i' the *Spence*, right pensivelie,
     I gaed to reſt.

   There, lanely, by the ingle-cheek,
I sat and ey'd the spewing reek,
That fill'd, wi' hoaſt-provoking smeek,
     The auld, clay biggin;
And heard the reſtless rattons squeak
     About the riggin.

* Duan, a term of Ossian's for the different divisions
of a digressive Poem. See his Cath-Loda, vol.2. of
McPherson's Translation.

All in this mottie, misty clime,
I backward mus'd on wasted time,
How I had spent my *youthfu' prime*,
    An' done nae-thing,
But stringing blethers up in rhyme
    For fools to sing.

Had I to guid advice but harket,
I might, by this, hae led a market,
Or strutted in a Bank and clarket
    My *Cash-Account*;
While here, half-mad, half-fed, half-sarket,
    Is a' th' amount.

I started, mutt'ring blockhead! coof!
And heav'd on high my wauket loof,
To swear by a' yon starry roof,
    Or some rash aith,
That I, henceforth, would be *rhyme-proof*
    Till my last breath—

When click! the *string* the *snick* did draw;
And jee! the door gaed to the wa';
And by my ingle-lowe I saw,
    Now bleezan bright,
A tight, outlandish *Hizzie,* braw,
    Come full in sight.

Ye need na doubt, I held my whisht;
The infant aith, half-form'd, was crusht;
I glowr'd as eerie's I'd been dusht,
    In some wild glen;
When sweet, like *modest Worth*, she blusht,
    And stepped ben.

Green, slender, leaf-clad *Holly-boughs*
Were twisted, gracefu', round her brows,
I took her for some SCOTTISH MUSE
    By that same token;
And come to stop those reckless vows,
    Would soon been broken.

A 'hare-brain'd, sentimental trace'
Was strongly marked in her face;
A wildly-witty, rustic grace
    Shone full upon her;
Her *eye*, ev'n turn'd on empty space,
    Beam'd keen with *Honor*.

Down flow'd her robe, a *tartan* sheen,
Till half a leg was scrimply seen;
And such a *leg!* my BESS, I ween,
    Could only peer it;
Sae straught, sae taper, tight and clean,
    Nane else came near it.

Her *Mantle* large, of greenish hue,
My gazing wonder chiefly drew;
Deep *lights* and *shades*, bold-mingling, threw
     A lustre grand;
And seem'd, to my astonish'd view,
     A *well-known* Land.

Here, rivers in the sea were lost;
There, mountains to the skies were tost:
Here, tumbling billows mark'd the coast,
     With surging foam;
There, distant shone, *Art's* lofty boast,
     The lordly dome.

Here, DOON pour'd down his far-fetch'd floods;
There, well-fed IRWINE stately thuds:
Auld, hermit AIRE staw thro' his woods,
     On to the shore;
And many a lesser torrent scuds,
     With seeming roar.

Low, in a sandy valley spread,
An ancient BOROUGH rear'd her head;
Still, as in *Scottish Story* read,
     She boasts a *Race*,
To ev'ry nobler virtue bred,
     And polish'd grace.

DUAN SECOND

With musing-deep, astonish'd stare,
I view'd the heavenly-seeming *Fair*;
A whisp'ring *throb* did witness bear
      Of kindred sweet,
When with an elder Sister's air
      She did me greet.

'All hail! *my own* inspired Bard!
'In me thy native Muse regard!
'Nor longer mourn thy fate is hard,
      'Thus poorly low!
'I come to give thee such *reward*,
      'As *we* bestow.

'Know, the great *Genius* of this Land,
Has many a light, aerial band,
'Who, all beneath his high command,
      'Harmoniously,
'As *Arts* or *Arms* they understand,
      'Their labors ply.

'They SCOTIA'S Race among them share;
'Some fire the *Sodger* on to dare;
'Some rouse the *Patriot* up to bare
  'Corruption's heart:
'Some teach the *Bard*, a darling care,
  'The tuneful Art.

 ''Mong swelling floods of reeking gore,
'They ardent, kindling spirits pour;
'Or, mid the venal Senate's roar,
  'They, sightless, stand,
'To mend the honest *Patriot-lore*,
  'And grace the hand.

 'Hence, FULLARTON, the brave and young;
'Hence, DEMPSTER'S truth-prevailing tongue;
'Hence, sweet harmonious BEATTIE sung
  'His 'Minstrel lays;'
'Or tore, with noble ardour stung,
  'The *Sceptic's* bays.

 'To lower Orders are assign'd,
'The humbler ranks of Human-kind,
'The rustic Bard, the lab'ring Hind,
  'The Artisan;
'All chuse, as, various they're inclin'd,
  'The various man.

'When yellow waves the heavy grain,
'The threat'ning *Storm*, some, ſtrongly, rein;
'Some teach to meliorate the plain,
    'With *tillage-skill*;
'And some inſtruct the Shepherd-train,
    'Blythe o'er the hill.

   'Some hint the Lover's harmless wile;
'Some grace the Maiden's artless smile;
'Some soothe the Lab'rer's weary toil,
    'For humble gains,
'And make his *cottage-scenes* beguile
    'His cares and pains.

   'Some, bounded to a diſtrict-space,
'Explore at large Man's *infant race*,
'To mark the embryotic trace,
    'Of *ruſtic Bard*;
'And careful note each op'ning grace,
    'A guide and guard.

   '*Of these am I* – COILA my name;
'And this diſtrict as mine I claim,
'Where once the *Campbell's*, chiefs of fame,
    'Held ruling pow'r:
'I mark'd thy embryo-tuneful flame,
    'Thy natal hour.

'With future hope, I oft would gaze,
'Fond, on thy little, early ways,
'Thy rudely-caroll'd, chiming phrase,
    'In uncouth rhymes,
'Fir'd at the simple, artless lays
    'Of other times.

  'I saw thee seek the founding shore,
'Delighted with the dashing roar;
'Or when the *North* his fleecy store
    'Drove thro' the sky,
'I saw grim Nature's visage hoar;
    'Struck thy young eye.

  'Or when the deep-green-mantl'd Earth,
'Warm-cherish'd ev'ry floweret's birth,
'And joy and music pouring forth,
    'In ev'ry grove,
'I saw thee eye the gen'ral mirth
    'With boundless love.

  'When ripen'd fields, and azure skies,
'Call'd forth the *Reaper's* rustling noise,
'I saw thee leave their ev'ning joys,
    'And lonely stalk,
'To vent thy bosom's swelling rise,
    'In pensive walk.

'When *youthful Love*, warm-blushing, strong,
'Keen-shivering shot thy nerves along,
'Those accents, grateful to thy tongue,
    'Th' adored *Name*,
'I taught thee how to pour in song,
    'To soothe thy flame.

  'I saw thy pulse's maddening play,
'Wild-send thee Pleasure's devious way,
'Misled by Fancy's *meteor-ray*,
    'By Passion driven;
'But yet the *light* that led astray,
    'Was *light* from Heaven.

  'I taught thy manners-painting strains,
'The *loves*, the *ways* of simple swains,
'Till now, o'er all my wide domains,
    'Thy fame extends;
'And some, the pride of *Coila's* plains
    'Become thy friends.

  'Thou canst not learn, nor I can show,
'To paint with *Thomson's* landscape-glow;
'Or wake the bosom-melting throe,
    'With *Shenstone's* art;
'Or pour, with *Gray*, the moving flow,
    'Warm on the heart.

'Yet all beneath th'unrivall'd Rose,
'The lowly Daisy sweetly blows;
'Tho' large the forest's Monarch throws
      'His army shade,
'Yet green the juicy Hawthorn grows,
      'Adown the glade.

'Then never murmur nor repine;
'Strive in thy *humble sphere* to shine;
'And trust me, not *Potosi's mine*,
      'Nor *Kings regard*,
'Can give a bliss o'ermatching thine,
      'A *rustic Bard*.

'To give my counsels all in one,
'Thy *tuneful flame* still careful fan;
'Preserve *the dignity of Man*,
      'With Soul erect;
'And trust, the UNIVERSAL PLAN
      'Will all protect.

'*And wear thou this*' — She solemn said,
And bound the *Holly* round my head:
'The polish'd leaves, and berries red,
      Did rustling play;
And, like a passing thought, she fled,
      In light away.

THE following POEM will, by many Readers, be well enough underſtood; but, for the sake of those who are unacquainted wíth the manners and tradítions of the country where the scene is caſt, Notes are added, to give some account of the principal Charms and Spells of that Night, so big wíth Prophecy to the Peasantry in the Weſt of Scotland. The passion of prying into Futuríty makes a ſtriking part of the hiſtory of Human-nature, in ít's rude ſtate, in all ages and nations; and ít may be some entertainment to a philo-sophic mind, if any such should honor the Author wíth a perusal, to see the remains of ít, among the more unenlightened in our own.

HALLOWEEN *

Yes! let the Rich deride, the Proud disdain,
The simple pleasures of the lowly train;
To me more dear, congenial to my heart,
One native charm, than all the gloss of art.

GOLDSMITH

I

UPON that *night*, when Fairies light,
   On *Cassilis Downans* † dance,
Or owre the lays, in splendid blaze,
   On sprightly coursers prance;
Or for *Colean*, the rout is taen,
   Beneath the moon's pale beams;
There, up the *Cove*, ‡ to ſtray an' rove,
   Amang the rocks an' ſtreams
      To sport that night.

* Is thought to be a night when Wîtches, Devils and
  other mischief-making beings, are all abroad on
  their baneful, midnight errands: particularly,
  those aerial people, the Fairies, are said, on that
  night, to hold a grand Anniversary.

† Certain lîttle, romantic, rocky, green hills, in the
  neighbourhood of the ancient seat of the Earls of
  Cassilis.

‡ A noted cavern near Colean-house, called the
  Cove of Colean; which, as well as Cassilis
  Downans, is famed, in country ſtory, for being a
  favourîte haunt of Fairies.

II

Amang the bonie, winding banks,
 Where *Doon* rins, wimplin, clear,
Where BRUCE † ance rul'd the martial ranks,
 An' shook his *Carrick* spear,
Some merry, friendly, countra folks,
 Together did convene,
To *burn* their nits, an' *pou* their stocks,
 An' haud their *Halloween*
   Fu' blythe that night.

III

The lasses feat, an' cleanly neat,
 Mair braw than when they're fine;
Their faces blythe, fu' sweetly kythe,
 Hearts leal, an' warm, an' kin':
The lads sae trig, wi' wooer-babs,
 Weel knotted on their garten,
Some unco blate, an' some wi' gabs,
 Gar lasses hearts gang startin
   Whyles fast at night.

† The famous family of that name, the ancestors of
 ROBERT, the great Deliverer of his country,
 were Earls of Carrick.

IV

Then, first an' foremost, thro' the kail,
   Their *stocks* * maun a' be sought ance;
They steek their een, an' grape an' wale,
   For muckle anes, an' straught anes.
Poor hav'rel *Will* fell aff the drift,
   An' wander'd thro' the *Bow-kail*,
An' pow't, for want o' better shift,
   A *runt* was like a sow-tail
      Sae bow't that night.

V

Then, straught or crooked, yird or nane,
   They roar an' cry a' throw'ther;

* The first ceremony of Halloween, is, pulling each
a *Stock*, or plant of kail. They must go out, hand in
hand, with eyes shut, and pull the first they meet
with: its being big or little, straight or crooked, is
prophetic of the size and shape of the grand
object of all their Spells — the husband or wife.
If any *yird*, or earth, stick to the root, that is *tocher*,
or fortune; and the taste of the *custoc*, that is, the
heart of the stem, is indicative of the natural
temper and disposition. Lastly, the stems, or to
give them their ordinary appellation, the *runts*,
are placed somewhere above the head of the door;
and the christian names of the people whom
chance brings into the house, are, according to
the priority of placing the *runts*, the names
in question.

The vera *wee-things*, toddlan, rin,
 Wi' ſtocks out owre their shouther:
An' gif the *cuſtock's* sweet or sour,
 Wi' joctelegs they taſte them;
Syne coziely, aboon the door,
 Wi' cannie care, they've plac'd them
  To lye that night.

VI

The lasses ſtaw frae 'mang them a',
 To pou their *ſtalks o' corn*; *
But *Rab* flips out, an' jinks about,
 Behint the muckle thorn:
He grippet *Nelly* hard an' faſt;
 Loud skirl'd a' the lasses;
But her *tap-pickle* maiſt was loſt,
 When kiutlan in the *Fause-house* †
  Wi' him that night.

* They go to the barn-yard, and pull each, at three
 several times, a ſtalk of Oats. If the third ſtalk
 wants the *top-pickle*, that is, the grain at the top of
 the ſtalk, the party in queſtion will want the
 Maidenhead.

† When the corn is in a doubtful ſtate, by being too
 green, or wet, the Stack-builder, by means of old
 timber, &c. makes a large apartment in his ſtack,
 with an opening in the side which is faireſt
 exposed to the wind: this he calls a *Fause-house*.

VII

The auld Guidwife's weel-hoordet nîts *
    Are round an' round divided,
An' monie lads an' lasses fates
    Are there that night decided:
Some kindle, couthie, side by side,
    An' *burn* thegîther trimly;
Some ſtart awa, wi' saucy pride,
    An' jump out owre the chimlie
        Fu' high that night.

VIII

Jean slips in twa, wi' tentie e'e;
    Wha 'twas, she wadna tell;
But this is *Jock*, an' this is *me*,
    She says in to hersel:
He bleez'd owre her, an' she owre him,
    As they wad never mair part,
Till fuff! he ſtarted up the lum,
    An' *Jean* had e'en a sair heart
        To see't that night.

* Burning the nuts is a favourîte charm. They name
the lad and lass to each particular nut, as they lay
them in the fire; and according as they burn
quietly together, or ſtart from beside one
another, the course and issue of the Courtship
will be.

IX

Poor Willie, wi' his *bow-kail runt*,
   Was *brunt* wi' primsie *Mallie;*
An' *Mary*, nae doubt, took the drunt,
   To be compar'd to *Willie:*
Mall's nît lap out, wi' pridefu' fling,
   An' her ain fît, ît brunt ît;
While *Willie* lap, an' swoor by *jing*,
   'Twas juſt the way he wanted
            To be that night.

X

Nell had the *Fause-house* in her min',
   She pîts hersel an' *Rob* in;
In loving bleeze they sweetly join,
   Till whîte in ase they're sobbin:
Nell's heart was dancin at the view;
   She whisper'd *Rob* to leuk for't:
Rob, ſtownlins, prie'd her bonie mou,
   Fu' cozie in the neuk for't,
            Unseen that night.

XI

But *Merran* sat behint their backs,
   Her thoughts on *Andrew Bell*;
She lea'es them gashan at their cracks,

An' slips out by hersel:
She thro' the yard the nearest taks,
    An' for the *kiln* she goes then,
An' darklins grapet for the *bauks*,
    And in the *blue-clue* * throws then,
        Right fear't that night.

XII

An' ay she *win't* an' ay she swat,
    I wat she made nae jaukin;
Till something *held* within the *pat*,
    Guid L—d! but she was quaukin!
But whether 'twas the *Deil* himsel,
    Or whether 'twas a *bauk-en'*,
Or whether it was *Andrew Bell*,
    She did na wait on talkin
        To spier that night.

* Whoever would, with success, try this spell, must
strictly observe these directions. Steal out, all
alone, to the *kiln*, and, darkling, throw into the
pot, a clew of blue yarn: wind it in a new clew off
the old one; and towards the latter end, something
will hold the thread: demand, *wha hauds*? ie. who
holds? and answer will be returned from the kiln-
pot, by naming the christian and sirname of your
future Spouse.

XIII

Wee *Jenny* to her Graunie says,
   'Will ye go wi' me Graunie?
'I'll *eat the apple* * at the *glass*,
   'I gat frae uncle Johnie:'
She fuff't her pipe wi' sic a lunt,
   In wrath she was sae vap'rin,
She notic't na, an aizle brunt
    Her braw, new, worset apron
       Out thro' that night.

XIV

'Ye little Skelpie-limmer's-face!
   'I daur you try sic sportin,
'As seek the *foul Thief* onie place,
   'For him to spae your fortune:
'Nae doubt but ye may get a *sight*!
   'Great cause ye hae to fear it;
'For monie a ane has gotten a fright,
   'An' liv'd an' di'd deleeret,
      'On sic a night.

* Take a candle, and go, alone, to a looking glass:
  eat an apple before it, and some traditions say you
  should comb your hair all the time: the face of
  your conjugal companion, *to be*, will be seen in the
  glass, as if peeping over your shoulder.

XV

'Ae Hairſt afore the *Sherra-moor*,
   'I mind't as weel's yeſtreen,
'I was a gilpey then, I'm sure,
   'I was na paſt fyfteen:
'The Simmer had been cauld an' wat,
   'An' *Stuff* was unco green;
'An' ay a rantan *Kirn* we gat,
   'An' juſt on *Halloween*
        'It fell that night.

XVI

'Our *Stibble-rig* was *Rab M'Graen*,
   'A clever, ſturdy fallow;
'His Sin gat *Eppie Sim* wi' wean,
   'That liv'd in Achmacalla:
'He gat *hemp-seed*, * I mind ît weel,

* Steal out, unperceived, and sow a handful of
  hemp seed; harrowing ît wîth any thing you can
  conveniently draw after you. Repeat, now and
  them, 'Hemp seed I saw thee, Hemp 'seed I saw
  thee; and him (or her) that is to be my true-love,
  'come after me and pou thee.' Look over your left
  shoulder, and you will see the appearance of the
  person invoked, in the attîtude of pulling hemp.
  Some tradîtions say, 'come after 'me and shaw
  thee,' that is, show thyself; in which case ît simply
  appears. Others omît the harrowing, and say,
  'come after me and harrow thee.'

'An' he made unco light o't;
'But monie a day was *by himsel*,
   'He was sae sairly frighted
      'That vera night.'

XVII

Then up gat fechtan *Jamie Fleck*,
   An' he swoor by his conscience,
That he could *saw hemp-seed* a peck;
   For it was a' but nonsense:
The auld guidman raught down the pock,
   An' out a handfu' gied him;
Syne bad him slip frae 'mang the folk,
   Sometime when nae ane see'd him,
      An' try't that night.

XVIII

He marches thro' amang the stacks,
   Tho' he was something sturtan;
The *graip* he for a *harrow* taks,
   An' haurls at his curpan:
And ev'ry now an' then, he says,
   'Hemp-seed I saw thee,
'An' her that is to be my lass,
   'Come after me an' draw thee
      'As fast this night.'

XIX

He whiſtl'd up *lord Lenox' march*,
　　To keep his courage cheary;
Altho' his hair began to arch,
　　He was sae fley'd an' eerie:
Till presently he hears a squeak,
　　An' then a grane an' gruntle;
He by his showther gae a keek,
　　An' tumbl'd wi' a wintle
　　　　　Out owre that night.

XX

He roar'd a horrid murder-shout,
　　In dreadfu' desperation!
An' young an' auld come rinnan out,
　　An' hear the sad narration:
He swoor 'twas hilchan *Jean M'Craw*,
　　Or crouchie *Merran Humphie*,
Till ſtop! she trotted thro' them a';
　　An' wha was ît but *Grumphie*
　　　　　Aſteer that night?

XXI

Meg fain wad to the *Barn* gaen,
    To *winn three wechts o' naething*; *
But for to meet the Deil her lane,
    She pat but little faith in:
She gies the Herd a pickle nits,
    An' twa red cheeket apples,
To watch, while for the *Barn* she sets,
    In hopes to see *Tam Kipples*
            That vera night.

XXII

She turns the key, wi' cannie thraw,
    An' owre the threshold ventures;
But first on *Sawnie* gies a ca',
    Syne bauldly in she enters:

* This charm must likewise be performed,
  unperceived and alone. You go to the *barn*, and
  open both doors; taking them off the hinges, if
  possible; for there is danger, that the Being,
  about to appear, may shut the doors, and do you
  some mischief. Then take that instrument used in
  winnowing the corn, which, in our country-
  dialect, we call a *wecht*, and go thro' all the
  attitudes of letting down corn against the wind.
  Repeat it three times; and the third time, an
  apparition will pass thro' the barn, in at the windy
  door, and out at the other, having both the figure
  in question and the appearance or retinue,
  marking the employment or station in life.

A *ratton* rattl'd up the wa',
 An' she cry'd, L—d preserve her!
An' ran thro' midden-hole an' a',
 An' pray'd wi' zeal and fervour,
   Fu' faſt that night.

XXIII

They hoy't out Will, wi' fair advice;
 They hecht him some fine braw ane;
It chanc'd the *Stack* he *faddom't thrice,* *
 Was timmer-propt for thrawin:
He taks a swirlie, auld *moss-oak,*
 For some black, grousome *Carlin*;
An' loot a winze, an' drew a ſtroke,
 Till skin in blypes cam haurlin
   Aff's nieves that night.

XXIV

A wanton widow *Leezie* was,
 As cantie as a kîttlen;
But Och! that night, amang the shaws,
 She gat a fearfu' settlin!

* Take an opportunîty of going, unnoticed, to a
Bear-ſtack, and fathom ît three times round. The
laſt fathom of the laſt time, you will catch in your
arms, the appearance of your future conjugal
yoke-fellow.

She thro' the whins, an' by the cairn,
   An' owre the hill gaed scrievin,
Whare *three Lairds' lan's met at a burn,* *
   To dip her *left sark-sleeve* in,
            Was bent that night.

XXV

Whyles owre a linn the burnie plays,
   As thro' the glen it wimpl't;
Whyles round a rocky scar it ſtrays;
   Whyles in a wiel it dimpl't;
Whyles glitter'd to the nightly rays,
   Wi' bickerin, dancin dazzle;
Whyles cooket underneath the braes,
   Below the spreading hazle
            Unseen that night.

XXVI

Amang the brachens, on the brae,
   Between her an' the moon,

---

* You go out, one or more, for this is a social spell,
  to a south-running spring or rivulet, where 'three
  Lairds' lands 'meet,' and dip your left shirt-
  sleeve. Go to bed in sight of a fire, and hang your
  wet sleeve before it to dry. Ly awake; and
  sometime near midnight, an apparition, having
  the exact figure of the grand object in queſtion,
  will come and turn the sleeve, as if to dry the
  other side of it.

The Deil, or else an outler Quey,
   Gat up an' gae a croon:
Poor *Leezie's* heart maiſt lap the hool;
   Near lav'rock-height she jumpet.
But miſt a fiſt, an' in the *pool*,
   Out owre the lugs she plumpet,
      Wi' a plunge that night.

XXVII

In order, on the clean hearth-ſtane,
   The *Luggies* * three are ranged;
And ev'ry time great care is taen,
   To see them duely changed:
Auld, uncle *John*, wha *wedlock's joys*,
   Sin' *Mar's-year* did desire,
Because he gat the toom dish thrice,
   He heav'd them on the fire,
      In wrath that night.

* Take three dishes; put clean water in one,
  foul water in another, and leave the third empty:
  blindfold a person, and lead him to the hearth
  where the dishes are ranged; he (or she) dips the
  left hand: if by chance in the clean water, the
  future husband or wife will come to the bar of
  Matrimony, a Maid; if in the foul, a widow; if in
  the empty dish, ît foretells, wîth equal certainty,
  no marriage at all. It is repeated three times;
  and every time the arrangement of the dishes is
  altered.

XXVIII

Wi' merry sangs, an' friendly cracks,
    I wat they did na weary;
And unco tales, an' funnie jokes,
    Their sports were cheap an' cheary:
Till *butter'd So'ns*, * wi' fragrant lunt,
    Set a' their gabs a ſteerin;
Syne, wi' a social glass o' ſtrunt,
      They parted aff careerin
          Fu' blythe that night.

* Sowens, wĭth butter inſtead of milk to them, is
always the *Halloween Supper*.

THE AULD FARMER'S NEW-YEAR-MORNING SALUTATION TO HIS AULD MARE, MAGGIE, ON GIVING HER THE ACCUSTOMED RIPP OF CORN TO HANSEL IN THE NEW-YEAR

A *Guid New-year* I wish you Maggie!
    Hae, there's a ripp to thy auld baggie:
Tho' thou's howe-backet, now, an' knaggie,
        I've seen the day,
Thou could hae gaen like ony staggie
        Out owre the lay.

  Tho' now thou's dowie, stiff an' crazy,
An' thy auld hide as white's a daisie,
I've seen thee dappl't, sleek an' glaizie,
        A bonie gray:
He should been tight that daur't to *raize* thee
        Ance in a day.

  Thou ance was i' the foremost rank,
A *filly* buirdly, steeve an' swank,
An' set weel down a shapely shank,
        As e'er tread yird;
An' could hae flown out owre a stank,
        Like onie bird.

It's now some nine-an'-twenty-year,
Sin' thou was my *Guidfather's Meere;*
He gied me thee, o' tocher clear,
  An' fifty mark;
Tho' it was sma', 'twas *weel–won* gear,
  An' thou was stark.

When first I gaed to woo my *Jenny,*
Ye then was trottan wi' your Minnie:
Tho' ye was trickie, slee an' funnie,
  Ye ne'er was donsie;
But hamely, tawie, quiet an' cannie
  An' unco sonsie.

That *day,* ye pranc'd wi' muckle pride,
When ye bure hame my bonie *Bride:*
An' sweet an' gracefu' she did ride
  Wi' maiden air!
KYLE-STEWART I could bragged wide,
  For sic a *pair.*

Tho' now ye dow but hoyte and hoble,
An' wintle like a saumont-coble,
That day, ye was a jinker noble,
  For heels an' win'!
An' ran them till they a' did wauble,
  Far, far behin'!

When thou an' I were young an' skiegh,
An' *Stable-meals* at Fairs were driegh,
How thou wad prance, an' snore, an' scriegh,
    An' tak the road!
Towns-bodies ran, an' stood abiegh,
    An' ca't thee mad.

When thou was corn't, an' I was mellow,
We took the road ay like a Swallow:
At *Brooses* thou had ne'er a fellow,
    For pith an' speed;
But ev'ry tail thou pay't them hollow,
    Whare'er thou gaed.

The sma', droot-rumpl't, hunter cattle,
Might aiblins waur't thee for a brattle;
But *sax Scotch mile*, thou try't their mettle,
    An' gart them whaizle:
Nae whip nor spur, but just a wattle
    O' saugh or hazle.

Thou was a noble *Fittie-lan'*,
As e'er in tug or tow was drawn!
Aft thee an' I, in aught hours gaun,
    On guid March-weather,
Hae turn'd *sax rood* beside our han',
    For days thegither.

Thou never braing't, an' fetch't, an' flisket,
But thy *auld tail* thou wad hae whisket,
An' spread abreed thy weel-fill'd *brisket*,
      Wi' pîth an' pow'r,
Till sprîttie knowes wad rair't an' risket
      An' slypet owre.

When frosts lay lang, an' snaws were deep,
An' threaten'd *labor* back to keep,
I gied thy *cog* a wee-bît heap
      Aboon the timmer;
I ken'd my *Maggie* wad na sleep
      For that, or Simmer.

In *cart* or *car* thou never reestet;
The steyest brae thou wad hae fac't ît;
Thou never lap, an' sten't, an' breastet,
      Then stood to blaw;
But just thy step a wee thing hastet,
      Thou snoov't awa.

My Pleugh is now thy *bairn-time* a';
Four gallant brutes, as e'er did draw;
Forby sax mae, I've sell't awa,
      That thou hast nurst:
They drew me thretteen pund an' twa,
      The vera warst.

Monie a fair daurk we twa hae wrought,
An' wi' the weary warl' fought!
An' monie an' *anxious day*, I thought
    We wad be beat!
Yet here to *crazy Age* we're brought,
    Wi' something yet.

An' think na, my auld, truſty *Servan'*,
That now perhaps thou's less deservin,
An' thy *auld days* may end in ſtarvin',
    For my laſt fow,
A heapet *Stimpart*, I'll reserve ane
    Laid by for you.

We've worn to crazy years thegîther;
We'll toyte about wi' ane anîther;
Wi' tentie care I'll flît thy tether,
    To some hain'd rig,
Whare ye may nobly rax your leather,
    Wi' sma' fatigue.

THE

COTTER'S

SATURDAY NIGHT

INSCRIBED TO R.A****, Esq;

Let not Ambition mock their useful toil,
Their homely joys, and destiny obscure;
Nor Grandeur hear, with a disdainful smile,
The short and simple annals of the Poor.

GRAY

I

MY lov'd, my honor'd, much respected
    friend,
  No mercenary Bard his homage pays;
With honest pride, I scorn each selfish end,
  My dearest meed, a friend's esteem and praise:
To you I sing in simple Scottish lays,
    The *lowly train* in life's sequester'd scene;
The native feelings strong, the guileless ways,
  What A**** in a *Cottage* would have been;
Ah! Tho' his worth unknown, far happier
    there I ween!

II

November chill blaws loud wi' angry sugh;
    The short'ning winter-day is near a close;
The miry beasts retreating frae the pleugh;
    The black'ning trains o' craws to their repose:
The toil-worn COTTER frae his labor goes,
    This night his weekly moil is at an end,
Collects his *spades*, his *mattocks* and his *hoes*,
    Hoping the *morn* in ease and rest to spend,
And weary, o'er the moor, his course does
        hameward bend.

III

At length his lonely *Cot* appears in view,
    Beneath the shelter of an aged tree;
The expectant *wee-things*, toddlan, stacher through
    To meet their *Dad*, wi' flichterin noise and glee.
His wee-bit ingle, blinkan bonilie,
    His clean hearth-stane, his thrifty *Wifie's* smile,
The *lisping infant*, prattling on his knee,
    Does a' his weary *kiaugh* and care beguile,
And makes him quite forget his labor and his toil.

VI

Belyve, the *elder bairns* come drapping in,
    At *Service* out, amang the Farmers roun';
Some ca' the pleugh, some herd, some tentie rin
    A cannie errand to a neebor town:
Their eldest hope, their *Jenny*, woman-grown,
    In youthfu' bloom, Love sparkling in her e'e,
Comes hame, perhaps, to shew a braw new gown,
    Or deposite her sair-won penny-fee,
To help her *Parents* dear, if they in hardship be.

V

With joy unfeign'd, *brothers* and *sisters* meet,
    And each for other's weelfare kindly spiers:
The social hours, swift-wing'd, unnotic'd fleet;
    Each tells the uncos that he sees or hears.
The Parents partial eye their hopeful years;
    Anticipation forward points the view;
The *Mother*, wi' her needle and her sheers,
    Gars auld claes look amaist as weel's the new;
The *Father* mixes a' wi' admonition due.

VI

Their Master's and their Mistress's command,
　　The *youngkers* a' are warned to obey;
And mind their labors wi' an eydent hand,
　　And ne'er, tho' out o' sight, to jauk or play:
'And O! be sure to fear the LORD alway!
　　'And mind your *duty*, duely, morn and night!
'Lest in temptation's path ye gang astray,
　　'Implore his *counsel* and assisting *might*:
'They never sought in vain that sought the
　　　　LORD aright.'

VII

But hark! a rap comes gently to the door;
　　Jenny, wha kens the meaning o' the same,
Tells how a neebor lad came o'er the moor,
　　To do some errands, and convoy her hame.
The wily Mother sees the *conscious flame*
　　Sparkle in *Jenny's* e'e, and flush her cheek,
With heart-struck, anxious care enquires his name,
　　While *Jenny* hafflins is afraid to speak;
Weel-pleas'd the Mother hears, it's nae wild,
　　　　worthless *Rake*.

VIII

With kindly welcome, *Jenny* brings him ben;
    A *ſtrappan youth*; he takes the Mother's eye;
Blythe *Jenny* sees the *viſit's* no ill taen;
    The Father cracks of horses, pleughs and kye.
The *Youngſter's* artless heart o'erflows wi' joy,
    But blate and laîthfu', scarce can weel behave;
The Mother, wi' a woman's wiles, can spy
    What makes the *youth* sae bashfu' and sae grave;
Weel-pleas'd to think her *bairn's* respected like the lave.

IX

O happy love! where love like this is found!
    O heart-felt raptures! bliss beyond compare!
I've paced much this weary, *mortal round*,
    And sage EXPERIENCE bids me this declare—
'If Heaven a draught of heavenly pleasure spare,
    'One *cordial* in this melancholy *Vale*,
''Tis when a youthful, loving, *modeſt* Pair,
    'In other's arms, breathe out the tender tale,
'Beneath the milk-whîte thorn that scents
        the ev'ning gale.'

X

Is there, in human form, that bears a heart —
    A Wretch! a Villain! loſt to love and truth!
That can, with ſtudied, sly, ensnaring art,
    Betray sweet Jenny's unsuspecting youth?
Curse on his perjur'd arts! dissembling smooth!
    Are *Honor*, *Virtue*, *Conscience*, all exil'd?
Is there no Pĩty, no relenting Ruth,
    Points to the Parents fondling o'er their Child?
Then paints the *ruin'd Maid*, and *their* diſtraction wild!

XI

But now the Supper crowns their simple board,
    The healsome *Porrĩtch*, chief of SCOTIA'S food:
The soupe their *only Hawkie* does afford,
    That 'yont the hallan snugly chows her cood:
The *Dame* brings forth, in complimental mood,
    To grace the lad, her weel-hain'd kebbuck, fell,
And aft he's preſt, and aft he ca's ĩt guid;
    The frugal *Wifie*, garrulous, will tell,
How 'twas a towmond auld, sin' Lint was i' the bell.

XII

The chearfu' Supper done, wi' serious face,
    They, round the ingle, form a circle wide;
The Sire turns o'er, with patriarchal grace,
    The big *ha'-Bible*, ance his *Father's* pride:
His bonnet rev'rently is laid aside,
    His *lyart haffets* wearing thin and bare;
Those ſtrains that once did sweet in ZION glide,
    He wales a portion with judicious care;
'*And let us worship GOD!*' he says with solemn air.

XIII

They chant their artless notes in simple guise;
    They tune their *hearts*, by far the nobleſt aim:
Perhaps *Dundee's* wild warbling measures rise,
    Or plaintive *Martyrs,* worthy of the name;
Or noble *Elgin* beets the heaven-ward flame,
    The sweeteſt far of SCOTIA'S holy lays:
Compar'd with these, *Italian trills* are tame;
    The tickl'd ears no heart-felt raptures raise;
Nae unison hae they, with our CREATOR'S praise.

XIV

The priest-like Father reads the sacred page,
 How *Abram* was the Friend of GOD on high;
Or, *Moses* bade eternal warfare wage,
 With *Amalek's* ungracious progeny;
Or how the *royal Bard* did groaning lye,
 Beneath the stroke of Heaven's avenging ire;
Or *Job's* pathetic plaint, and wailing cry;
 Or rapt *Isaiah's* wild, seraphic fire;
Or other *Holy Seers* that tune the *sacred lyre*.

XV

Perhaps the *Christian Volume* is the theme,
 How *guiltless blood* for *guilty man* was shed;
How HE, who bore in heaven the second name,
 Had not on Earth whereon to lay His head:
How His first *followers* and *servants* sped;
 The *Precepts sage* they wrote to many a land:
How *he*, who lone in *Patmos* banished,
 Saw in the sun a mighty angel stand;
And heard great *Bab'lon's* doom pronounc'd by
  Heaven's command.

XVI

Then kneeling down to HEAVEN'S ETERNAL
      KING,
    The *Saint*, the *Father*, and the *Husband* prays:
Hope 'springs exulting on triumphant wing,' *
    That *thus* they all shall meet in future days:
There, ever bask in *uncreated rays*,
    No more to sigh, or shed the bitter tear,
Together hymning their CREATOR'S praise,
    In *such society*, yet still more dear;
While circling Time moves round in an eternal
      sphere.

XVII

Compar'd with *this*, how poor Religion's pride,
    In all the pomp of *method*, and of *art*,
When men display to congregations wide,
    Devotion's ev'ry grace, except the *heart*!
The POWER, incens'd, the Pageant will desert,
    The pompous strain, the sacredotal stole;
But haply, in some *Cottage* far apart,
    May hear, well pleas'd, the language of the *Soul*;
And in His *Book of Life* the Inmates poor enroll.

* Pope's Windsor Forest.

XVIII

Then homeward all take off their sev'ral way;
    The youngling *Cottagers* retire to rest:
The Parent-pair their *secret homage* pay,
    And proffer up to Heaven the warm request,
That HE who stills the *raven's* clam'rous nest,
    And decks the *lily* fair in flow'ry pride,
Would, in the way *His Wisdom* sees the best,
    For *them* and for their *little ones* provide;
But chiefly, in their hearts with *Grace divine* preside.

XIX

From scenes like these, old SCOTIA'S grandeur
      springs.
    That makes her lov'd at home, rever'd abroad:
Princes and lords are but the breath of kings,
    'An honest man's the noble work of GOD;'
And *certes*, in fair Virtue's heavenly road,
    The *Cottage* leaves the *Palace* far behind:
What is a lordling's pomp? a cumbrous load,
    Disguising oft the *wretch* of human kind,
Studied in arts of Hell, in wickedness refin'd!

XX

O SCOTIA! my dear, my native soil!
  For whom my warmeſt wish to heaven is sent!
Long may thy hardy sons of *ruſtic toil*,
  Be bleſt wîth health, and peace, and sweet content!
And O may Heaven their simple lives prevent
  From *Luxury's* contagion, weak and vile!
Then howe'er *crowns* and *coronets* be rent,
  A *virtuous Populace* may rise the while,
And ſtand a wall of fire around their much-lov'd
    ISLE.

XXI

O THOU! who pour'd the *patriotic tide*,
  That ſtream'd thro' great, unhappy WALLACE'
    heart;
Who dar'd to, nobly, ſtem tyrannic pride,
  Or *nobly die*, the second glorious part:
(The Patriot's GOD, peculiarly thou art,
  His *friend, inſpirer, guardian* and *reward!*)
O never, never SCOTIA'S realm desert,
  But ſtill the *Patriot*, and the *Patriot-Bard*,
In bright succession raise, her *Ornament* and *Guard!*

TO A

MOUSE

On turning her up in her Nest, with the Plough,

November 1785

WEE, sleeket, cowran, tim'rous *beastie*,
O, what a panic's in thy breastie!
Thou need na start awa sae hasty,
Wi' bickering brattle!
I wad be laith to rin an' chase thee,
Wi' murd'ring *pattle*!

I'm truly sorry Man's dominion
Has broken Nature's social union,
An' justifies that ill opinion,
Which makes thee startle,
At me, thy poor, earth-born companion,
An' *fellow-mortal*!

I doubt na, whyles, but thou may *thieve*;
What then? poor beastie, thou maun live!
A *daimen-icker* in a *thrave*
'S a sma' request:
I'll get a blessin wi' the lave,
An' never miss't!

Thy wee-bit *housie* too, in ruin!
It's silly wa's the win's are ſtrewin!
An' naething, now, to big a new ane,
   O' foggage green!
An' bleak *December's winds* ensuin,
   Baîth snell an' keen!

 Thou saw the fields laid bare an' waſt,
An' weary *Winter* comin faſt,
An' cozie here, beneath the blaſt,
   Thou thought to dwell,
Till crash! the cruel *coulter* paſt
   Out thro' thy cell.

 That wee-bît heap o' leaves an' ſtibble,
Has coſt thee monie a weary nibble
Now thou's turn'd out, for a' thy trouble,
   But house or hald,
To thole the Winter's *sleety dribble*,
   An' *cranreuch* cauld!

But Mousie, thou art no thy-lane,
In proving *foresight* may be vain:
The best laid schemes o' *Mice* an' *Men*,
      Gang aft agley,
An' lea'e us nought but grief an' pain,
      For promis'd joy!

Still, thou art blest, compar'd wi' *me!*
The *present* only toucheth thee:
But Och! I *backward* cast my e'e,
      On prospects drear!
An' *forward*, tho' I canna *see*,
      I *guess* an' *fear!*

EPISTLE TO DAVIE,

A

BROTHER POET

January —

I

WHILE winds frae off BEN-
LOMOND blaw,
And bar the doors wi' driving snaw,
    And hing us owre the ingle,
I set me down, to pass the time,
And spin a verse or twa o' rhyme,
    In hamely, *westlin* jingle.
While frosty winds blaw in the drift,
    Ben to the chimla lug,
I grudge a wee the *Great-folk's* gift,
    That live sae bien an' snug:
        I tent less, and want less
            Their roomy fire-side;
        But hanker, and canker,
            To see their cursed pride.

II

It's hardly in a body's pow'r,
To keep, at times, frae being sour,
   To see how things are shar'd;
How *best o' chiels* are whyles in want,
While *Coofs* on countless thousands rant,
   And ken na how to wair't:
But DAVIE lad, ne'er fash your head,
   Tho' we hae little gear,
We're fit to win our daily bread,
   As lang's we're hale and fier:
      'Mair spier na, nor fear na,' *
        Auld age ne'er mind a feg;
      The last o't, the warst o't,
        Is only but to beg.

III

To lye in kilns and barns at e'en,
When banes are craz'd, and bluid is thin,
   Is, doubtless, great distress!
Yet then *content* could make us blest;
Ev'n then, sometimes we'd snatch a taste
   Of truest happiness.

* Ramsay.

The honeſt heart that's free frae a'
　　Intended fraud or guile,
However Fortune kick the ba',
　　　Has ay some cause to smile:
　　　　And mind ſtill, you'll find ſtill,
　　　　　A comfort this nae sma';
　　　　Nae mair then, we'll care then,
　　　　　Nae *farther* we can *fa'*.

IV

What tho', like Commoners of air,
We wander out, we know not where,
　　But eiſher house or hal'?
Yet *Nature's* charms, the hills and woods,
The sweeping vales, and foaming floods,
　　Are free alike to all.
In days when Daisies deck the ground,
　　And Blackbirds whiſtle clear,
With honeſt joy, our hearts will bound,
　　To see the *coming* year:
　　　　On braes when we please then,
　　　　　We'll ſit and *sowth* a tune;
　　　　Syne *rhyme* till't, we'll time till't,
　　　　　And sing't when we hae done.

V

It's no in titles nor in rank;
It's no in wealth like *Lon'on Bank,*
    To purchase peace and rest;
It's no in makin muckle, *mair*:
It's no in books; it's no in Lear,
    To make us truly blest:
If Happiness hae not her seat
    And center in the breast,
We may be *wise*, or *rich*, or *great*,
    But never can be *blest*:
        Nae treasures, nor pleasures
            Could make us happy lang;
        The *heart* ay's the part ay,
            That makes us right or wrang.

VI

Think ye, that sic as *you* and *I*,
Wha drudge and drive thro' wet and dry,
    Wi' never-ceasing toil;
Think ye, are we less blest than they,
Wha scarcely tent us in their way,
    As hardly worth their while?
Alas! how aft, in haughty mood,
    GOD'S creatures they oppress!

Or else, neglecting a' that's guid,
　　They riot in excess!
　　　　Baíth careless, and fearless,
　　　　　　Of eíther Heaven or Hell;
　　　　Eſteeming, and deeming,
　　　　　　It a' an idle tale!

VII

Then let us chearfu' acquiesce;
Nor make our scanty Pleasures less,
　　By pining at our ſtate:
And, ev'n should Misfortunes come,
I, here wha ſît, hae met wi' some,
　　An's thankfu' for them yet.
They gie the wít of *Age* to *Youth*;
　　They let us ken oursel;
They make us see the naked truth,
　　The *real* guid and ill.
　　　　Tho' losses, and crosses,
　　　　　　Be lessons right severe,
　　　　There's *wít* there, ye'll get there,
　　　　　　Ye'll find nae other where.

VIII

But tent me, DAVIE, *Ace o' Hearts*!
(To say aught less wad wrang the *cartes*,
    And flatt'ry I detest)
This life has joys for you and I;
And joys that riches ne'er could buy;
    And joys the very best,
There's a' the *Pleasures o' the Heart*,
    The *Lover* and the *Frien'*;
Ye hae your MEG, your dearest part,
    And I my darling JEAN!
        It warms me, it charms me,
           To mention but her *name*:
        It heats me, it beets me,
           And sets me a' on flame!

IX

O, all ye *Pow'rs* who rule above!
O THOU, whose very self art *love*!
    THOU know'st my words sincere!
The *life blood* streaming thro' my heart,
Or my more dear *Immortal part*,
    Is not more fondly dear!
When heart-corroding care and grief
    Deprive my soul of rest,
Her dear idea brings relief,

And solace to my breaſt.
  Thou BEING, Allseeing,
   O hear my fervent pray'r!
 Still take her, and make her,
   THY moſt peculiar care!

X

All hail! ye tender feelings dear!
The smile of love, the friendly tear,
 The sympathetic glow!
Long since, this world's thorny ways
Had number'd out my weary days,
 Had ît not been for you!
Fate ſtill has bleſt me wîth a friend,
 In ev'ry care and ill;
And oft a more *endearing* band,
 A *tye* more tender ſtill.
  It lightens, ît brightens,
   The tenebrific scene,
  To meet wîth, and greet wîth,
   My DAVIE or my JEAN!

XI

O, how that *name* inspires my ſtyle!
The words come skelpan, rank and file,
 Amaiſt before I ken!
The ready measure rins as fine,
As *Phœbus* and the famous *Nine*
 Were glowran owre my pen.
My spavet *Pegasus* will limp,
 Till ance he's fairly het;
And then he'll hilch, and ſtilt, and jimp,
 And rin an unco fit:
  But leaſt then, the beaſt then,
   Should rue this haſty ride,
  I'll light now, and dight now,
   His sweaty, wizen'd hide.

THE
LAMENT

OCCASIONED BY THE UNFORTUNATE ISSUE
OF A FRIEND'S AMOUR

Alas! how oft does goodness wound itself!
And sweet Affection *prove the spring of Woe!*

HOME

I

O Thou pale Orb, that silent shines,
    While care-untroubled mortals sleep!
Thou seest a *wretch*, who inly pines,
    And wanders here to wail and weep!
With Woe I nightly vigils keep,
    Beneath thy wan, unwarming beam;
And mourn, in lamentation deep,
    How *life* and *love* are all a dream!

II

I joyless view thy rays adorn,
    The faintly-marked, distant hill:
I joyless view thy trembling horn,
    Reflected in the gurgling rill.

My fondly-fluttering heart, be ſtill!
    Thou busy pow'r, Remembrance, cease!
Ah! muſt the agonizing thrill,
    For ever bar returning Peace!

III

No idly-feign'd, poetic pains,
    My sad, lovelorn lamentings claim:
No shepherd's pipe — Arcadian ſtrains;
    No fabled tortures, quaint and tame.
The *plighted faith*; the *mutual flame*;
    The *oft-atteſted Powers above*;
The *promis'd Father's tender name*;
    These were the pledges of my love!

IV

Encircled in her clasping arms,
    How have the raptur'd moments flown!
How have I wish'd for Fortune's charms,
    For her dear sake, and her's alone!
And, muſt I think ît! is she gone,
    My secret-heart's exulting boaſt?
And does she heedless hear my groan?
    And is she ever, ever loſt?

V

Oh! can she bear so base a heart,
    So loſt to Honor, loſt to Truth.
As from the *fondeſt* lover part,
    The *plighted husband* of her youth?
Alas! Life's path may be unsmooth!
    Her way may lie thro' rough diſtress!
Then, who her pangs and pains will soothe,
    Her sorrows share and make them less?

VI

Ye winged Hours that o'er us paſt,
    Enraptur'd more, the more enjoy'd,
Your dear remembrance in my breaſt,
    My fondly-treasur'd thoughts employ'd.
That breaſt, how dreary now, and void,
    For her too scanty once of room!
Ev'n ev'ry *ray* of *Hope* deſtroy'd,
    And not a *Wish* to gild the gloom!

VII

The morn that warns th'approaching day,
    Awakes me up to toil and woe:
I see the hours, in long array,
    That I muſt suffer, lingering, slow.

Full many a pang, and many a throe,
    Keen Recollection's direful train,
Muſt wring my soul, ere Phoebus, low,
    Shall kiss the diſtant, weſtern main.

VIII

And when my nightly couch I try,
    Sore-harass'd out, wĭth care and grief,
My toil-beat nerves, and tear-worn eye,
    Keep watchings wĭth the nightly thief:
Or if I slumber, Fancy, chief,
    Reigns, hagard-wild, in sore afright:
Ev'n day, all-bĭtter, brings relief,
    From such a horror-breathing night.

IX

O! thou bright Queen, who, o'er th'expanse,
    Now higheſt reign'ſt, wĭth boundless sway!
Oft has thy silent-marking glance
    Observ'd us, fondly-wand'ring, ſtray!
The time, unheeded, sped away,
    While Love's *luxurious pulse* beat high,
Beneath thy silver-gleaming ray,
    To mark the mutual-kindling eye.

X

Oh! scenes in strong remembrance set!
 Scenes, never, never to return!
Scenes, if in stupor I forget,
 Again I feel, again I burn!
From ev'ry joy and pleasure torn,
 Life's weary vale I'll wander thro';
And hopeless, comfortless, I'll mourn
 A faithless woman's broken vow.

DESPONDENCY

AN ODE

I

O PPRESS'D with grief, oppress'd with care,
   A burden more than I can bear,
  I set me down and sigh:
O Life! Thou art a galling load,
Along a rough, a weary road,
   To wretches such as I!
Dim-backward as I cast my view,
   What sick'ning Scenes appear!
What Sorrows *yet* may pierce me thro',
   Too justly I may fear!
     Still caring, despairing,
       Must be my bitter doom;
     My woes here, shall close ne'er,
       But with the *closing tomb*!

II

Happy! ye sons of Busy-life,
Who, equal to the bustling strife,
   No other view regard!
Ev'n when the wished *end's* deny'd,

Yet while the busy *means* are ply'd,
 They bring their own reward:
Whilst I, a hope-abandon'd wight,
 Unfitted with an *aim*,
Meet ev'ry sad-returning night,
 And joyless morn the same.
  You, bustling and justling,
   Forget each grief and pain;
  I, listless, yet restless,
   Find ev'ry prospect vain.

III

How blest the Solitary's lot,
Who, all-forgetting, all-forgot,
 Within his humble cell,
The cavern wild with tangling roots,
Sits o'er his newly-gather'd fruits,
 Beside his crystal well!
Or haply, to his ev'ning thought,
 By unfrequented stream,
The *ways of men* are distant brought,
 A faint-collected dream:
  While praising, and raising
   His thoughts to Heaven on high,
  As wand'ring, meand'ring,
   He views the solemn sky.

IV

Than I, no *lonely Hermit* plac'd
Where never human footstep trac'd,
   Less fit to play the part,
The *lucky moment* to improve,
And *just* to stop, and *just* to move,
   With *self-respecting* art:
But ah! those pleasures, Loves and Joys,
   Which I too keenly taste,
The *Solitary* can despise,
   Can want, and yet be blest!
     He needs not, he heeds not,
      Or human love or hate;
     Whilst I here, must cry here,
      At perfidy ingrate!

V

Oh, enviable, early days,
When dancing thoughtless Pleasure's maze,
   To Care, to Guilt unknown!
How ill exchang'd for riper times,
To feel the follies, or the crimes,
   Of others, or my own!
Ye tiny elves that guiltless sport,
   Like linnets in the bush,

Ye little know the ills ye court,
When Manhood is your wish!
The losses, the crosses,
That *active man* engage;
The fears all, the tears all.
Of dim declining *Age*!

MAN WAS MADE TO MOURN,

A

DIRGE

I

WHEN chill November's surly blast
  Made fields and forests bare,
One ev'ning, as I wand'red forth,
  Along the banks of AIRE,
I spy'd a man, whose aged step
  Seem'd weary, worn with care;
His face was furrow'd o'er with years
  And hoary was his hair.

II

Young stranger, whither wand'rest thou?
  Began the rev'rend Sage;
Does thirst of wealth thy step constrain,
  Or youthful Pleasure's rage?
Or haply, prest with cares and woes,
  Too soon thou hast began,
To wander forth, with me, to mourn
  The miseries of Man.

III

The Sun that overhangs yon moors,
    Out-spreading far and wide,
Where hundreds labour to support
    A haughty lordling's pride;
I've seen yon weary winter-sun
    Twice forty times return;
And ev'ry time has added proofs,
    That Man was made to mourn.

IV

O Man! While in thy early years,
    How prodigal of time!
Mispending all thy precious hours,
    Thy glorious, youthful prime!
Alternate Follies take the sway;
    Licentious Passions burn;
Which tenfold force gives Nature's law,
    That Man was made to mourn.

V

Look not alone on youthful Prime,
    Or Manhood's active might;
Man then is useful to his kind,
    Supported is his right:

But see him on the edge of life,
    With Cares and Sorrows worn,
Then Age and Want, Oh! ill-match'd pair!
    Show Man was made to mourn.

VI

A few seem favourites of Fate,
    In Pleasure's lap careſt;
Yet, think not all the Rich and Great,
    Are likewise truly bleſt.
But Oh! what crouds in ev'ry land,
    All wretched and forlorn,
Thro' weary life this lesson learn,
    That Man was made to mourn!

VII

Many and sharp the num'rous Ills
    Inwoven with our frame!
More pointed ſtill we make ourselves,
    Regret, Remorse and Shame!
And Man, whose heav'n-erected face,
    The smiles of love adorn,
Man's inhumanity to Man
    Makes countless thousands mourn!

VIII

See, yonder poor, o'erlabour'd wight,
  So abject, mean and vile,
Who begs a brother of the earth
  To give him leave to toil;
And see his lordly *fellow-worm*,
  The poor petition spurn,
Unmindful, tho' a weeping wife,
  And helpless offspring mourn.

IX

If I'm design'd yon lordling's slave,
  By Nature's law design'd,
Why was an independent wish
  E'er planted in my mind?
If not, why am I subject to
  His cruelty, or scorn?
Or why has Man the will and pow'r
  To make his fellow mourn?

X

Yet, let not this too much, my Son,
  Disturb thy youthful breast:
This partial view of human-kind
  Is surely not the *last*!

The poor, oppressed, honeſt man
    Had never, sure, been born,
Had there not been some recompence
    To comfort those that mourn!

XI

O Death! the poor man's deareſt friend,
    The kindeſt and the beſt!
Welcome the hour, my aged limbs
    Are laid with thee at reſt!
The Great, the Wealthy fear thy blow,
    From pomp and pleasure torn;
But Oh! a bleſt relief for those
    That weary-laden mourn!

WINTER,

A

DIRGE

I

THE Wintry West extends his blast,
   And hail and rain does blaw;
Or, the stormy North sends driving forth,
   The blinding sleet and snaw:
While, tumbling brown, the Burn comes down,
   And roars frae bank to brae;
And bird and beast, in covert, rest,
   And pass the heartless day.

II

'The sweeping blast, the sky o'ercast,' *
   The joyless *winter-day*,
Let others fear, to me more dear,
   Than all the pride of May:
The Tempest's howl, it *soothes* my soul,
   My *griefs* it seems to join;
The leafless trees my fancy please,
   Their *fate* resembles mine!

* Dr. Young.

III

Thou POW'R SUPREME, whose mighty Scheme,
    These *woes* of mine fulfil;
Here, firm, I reſt, they *muſt* be beſt,
    Because they are *Thy* Will!
Then all I want (Oh, do thou grant
    This one requeſt of mine!)
Since to *enjoy* Thou doſt deny,
    Assiſt me to *resign*!

A

PRAYER,

IN THE PROSPECT OF DEATH

I

O THOU unknown, Almighty Cause
    Of all my hope and fear!
In whose dread Presence, ere an hour,
    Perhaps I must appear!

II

If I have wander'd in those paths
    Of life I ought to shun;
As *Something*, loudly, in my breast,
    Remonstrates I have done;

III

Thou know'st that Thou hast formed me;
    With Passions wild and strong;
And list'ning to their witching voice
    Has often led me wrong.

IV

Where human *weakness* has come short,
    Or *frailty* ſtept aside,
Do Thou, ALL-GOOD, for such Thou art,
    In shades of darkness hide.

V

Where wíth *intention* I have err'd,
    No other plea I have,
But, *Thou art good*; and Goodness ſtill
    Delighteth to forgive.

TO A
MOUNTAIN-
DAISY

On turning one down, with the Plough, in
April — 1786

WEE, modeſt, crimson-tipped flow'r,
    Thou's met me in an evil hour;
For I maun crush amang the ſtoure
      Thy slender ſtem:
To spare thee now is paſt my pow'r,
      Thou bonie gem.

    Alas! it's no thy neebor sweet,
The bonie *Lark*, companion meet!
Bending thee 'mang the dewy weet!
      Wi's spreckl'd breaſt,
When upward-springing, blythe, to greet
      The purpling Eaſt.

    Cauld blew the bitter-biting *North*
Upon thy early, humble birth;
Yet chearfully thou glinted forth
      Amid the ſtorm,
Scarce rear'd above the *Parent-earth*
      Thy tender form.

The flaunting *flow'rs* our Gardens yield,
High-shelt'ring woods and wa's maun shield,
But thou, beneath the random bield
      O' clod or ſtane,
Adorns the hiſtie *ſtibble-field*,
      Unseen, alane.

There, in thy scanty mantle clad,
Thy snawie bosom sun-ward spread,
Thou lifts thy unassuming head
      In humble guise;
But now the *share* uptears thy bed,
      And low thou lies!

Such is the fate of artless Maid,
Sweet *flow'ret* of the rural shade!
By Love's simplicity betray'd,
      And guileless truſt,
Till she, like thee, all foil'd, is laid
      Low i' the duſt.

Such is the fate of simple Bard,
On Life's rough ocean luckless ſtarr'd!
Unskilful he to note the card
      Of *prudent Lore*,
Till billows rage, and gales blow hard,
      And whelm him o'er!

Such fate *suffering worth* is giv'n,
Who long with wants and woes has striv'n,
By human pride or cunning driv'n
      To Mis'ry's brink,
Till wrench'd of ev'ry stay but HEAV'N,
      He, ruin'd, sink!

Ev'n thou who mourn'st the *Daisy's* fate,
That fate is thine — no distant date;
Stern Ruin's *plough-share* drives, elate,
      Full on thy bloom,
Till crush'd beneath the *furrows* weight,
      Shall be thy doom!

TO

R U I N

I

ALL hail! inexorable lord!
    At whose destruction-breathing word,
    The mightiest empires fall!
Thy cruel, woe-delighted train,
The ministers of Grief and Pain,
    A sullen welcome, all!
With stern-resolv'd, despairing eye,
    I see each aimed dart;
For one has cut my *dearest tye*,
    And quivers in my heart.
Then low'ring, and pouring,
    The *Storm* no more I dread;
Tho' thick'ning, and black'ning,
    Round my devoted head.

II

And thou grim Pow'r by Life abhorr'd,
While Life a *pleasure* can afford,
    Oh! hear a wretch's pray'r!
No more I shrink appall'd, afraid;
I court, I beg thy friendly aid,

To close this scene of care!
When shall my soul, in silent peace,
Resign Life's *joyless* day?
My weary heart it's throbbings cease,
Cold-mould'ring in the clay?
No fear more, no tear more,
To ſtain my lifeless face,
Enclasped, and grasped,
Within thy cold embrace!

EPISTLE

TO A

YOUNG FRIEND

May — 1786

I

I LANG hae thought, my youthfu' friend,
    A Something to have sent you,
Tho' it should serve nae other end
    Than just a kind memento;
But how the subject theme may gang,
    Let time and chance determine;
Perhaps it may turn out a Sang;
    Perhaps, turn out a Sermon.

II

Ye'll try the world soon my lad,
    And ANDREW dear believe me,
Ye'll find mankind an unco squad,
    And muckle they may grieve ye:
For care and trouble set your thought,
    Ev'n when your end's attained;
And a' your views may come to nought,
    Where ev'ry nerve is strained.

III

I'll no say, men are villains a';
　　The real, harden'd wicked,
Wha hae nae check but *human law*,
　　Are to a few reſtricked:
But Och, mankind are unco weak,
　　An' liꞔtle to be truſted;
If *Self* the wavering balance shake,
　　It's rarely right adjuſted!

IV

Yet they wha fa' in Fortune's ſtrife?
　　Their fate we should na censure,
For ſtill th' *important end* of life,
　　They equally may answer:
A man may hae an *honeſt heart*,
　　Tho' Poortiꞔth hourly ſtare him;
A man may tak a neebor's part,
　　Yet hae nae *cash* to spare him.

V

Ay free, aff han', your ſtory tell,
　　When wi' a bosom crony;
But ſtill keep something to yoursel
　　Ye scarcely tell to ony.

Conceal yoursel as weel's ye can
 Frae critical dissection;
But keek thro' ev'ry other man,
 Wi' sharpen'd, sly inspection.

VI

The *sacred lowe* o' weel plac'd love,
 Luxuriantly indulge it;
But never tempt th' *illicit rove*,
 Tho' naething should divulge it:
I wave the quantum o' the sin;
 The hazard of concealing;
But Och! it hardens *a' within*,
 And petrifies the feeling!

VII

To catch Dame Fortune's golden smile,
 Assiduous wait upon her;
And gather gear by ev'ry wile,
 That's justify'd by Honor:
Not for to *hide* it in a *hedge*,
 Nor for a *train-attendant*;
But for the glorious priviledge
 Of being *independant*.

VIII

The *fear o' Hell's* a hangman's whip,
    To haud the wretch in order;
But where ye feel your *Honor* grip,
    Let that ay be your border:
It's slightest touches, instant pause—
    Debar a' side-pretences;
And resolutely keep it's laws,
    Uncaring consequences.

IX

The great CREATOR to revere,
    Must sure become the *Creature*;
But still the preaching cant forbear,
    And ev'n the rigid feature:
Yet ne'er with Wits prophane to range,
    Be complaisance extended;
An *athiest-laugh's* a poor exchange
    For *Deity offended*!

X

When ranting round in Pleasure's ring,
    Religion may be blinded;
Or if she gie a *random-fling*,
    It may be little minded;

But when on Life we're tempest-driven,
    A Conscience but a canker—
A correspondence fix'd wi' Heav'n,
    Is sure a noble *anchor*!

XI

Adieu, dear, amiable Youth!
    Your *heart* can ne'er be wanting!
May Prudence, Fortitude and Truth
    Erect your brow undaunting!
In *ploughman phrase* 'GOD send you speed,'
    Still daily to grow wiser;
And may ye better reck the *rede*,
    Than ever did th' *Adviser*!

ON A

SCOTCH BARD

GONE TO THE WEST INDIES

A' YE wha live by sowps o' drink,
   A' ye wha live by crambo-clink,
A' ye wha live and never think,
      Come, mourn wi' me!
Our *billie's* gien us a' a jink,
      An' owre the Sea.

   Lament him a' ye rantan core,
Wha dearly like a random-splore;
Nae mair he'll join the *merry roar*,
      In social key;
For now he's taen anither shore,
      An' owre the Sea!

   The bonie lasses weel may wiss him,
And in their dear *petitions* place him:
The widows, wives, an' a' may bless him,
      Wi' tearfu' e'e;
For weel I wat they'll sairly miss him
      That's owre the Sea!

O Fortune, they hae room to grumble!
Hadst thou taen aff some drowsy bummle,
Wha can do nought but fyke an' fumble,
             'Twad been nae plea;
But he was gleg as onie wumble,
             That's owre the Sea!

Auld, cantie KYLE may weepers wear,
An' stain them wi' the saut, saut tear:
'Twill mak her poor, auld heart, I fear,
             In flinders flee:
He was her *Laureat* monie a year,
             That's owre the Sea!

He saw Misfortune's cauld *Nor-west*
Lang-mustering up a bitter blast;
A Jillet brak his heart at last,
             Ill may she be!
So, took a birth afore the mast,
             An' owre the Sea.

To tremble under Fortune's cummock,
On scarce a bellyfu' o' *drummock*,
Wi' his proud, independant stomach,
             Could ill agree;
So, row't his hurdies in a *hammock*,
             An' owre the Sea.

He ne'er was gien to great misguidin,
Yet coin his pouches wad na bide in;
Wi' him ît ne'er was *under hidin*;
  He dealt ît free:
The *Muse* was a' that he took pride in,
  That's owre the Sea.

Jamaica bodies, use him weel,
An' hap him in a cozie biel:
Ye'll find him ay a dainty chiel,
  An' fou o' glee:
He wad na wrang'd the vera *Diel*,
  That's owre the Sea.

Fareweel, my *rhyme-composing billie*!
Your native soil was right ill-willie;
But may ye flourish like a lily,
  Now bonilie!
I'll toaſt you in my hindmoſt *gillie*,
  Tho' owre the Sea!

A

DEDICATION

TO

G**** H******* Esq

EXPECT na, Sir, in this narration,
   A fleechan, fleth'ran *Dedication*,
To roose you up, an' ca' you guid,
An' sprung o' great an' noble bluid;
Because ye're sirnam'd like *His Grace*,
Perhaps related to the race:
Then when I'm tir'd — and sae are *ye*,
Wi' monie a fulsome, sinfu' lie,
Set up a face, how I stop short,
For fear your modesty be hurt.

   This may do — maun do, Sir, wi' them wha
Maun please the Great-folk for a wamefou;
For me! sae laigh I need na bow,
For, LORD be thanket, *I can plough*;
And when I downa yoke a naig,
Then, LORD be thanket, *I can beg*;
Sae I shall say, an' that's nae flatt'rin,
It's just *sic Poet* an' *sic Patron*.

The Poet, some guid Angel help him,
Or else, I fear, some *ill ane* skelp him!
He may do weel for a' he's done yet,
But only — he's no juſt begun yet.

The Patron, (Sir, ye maun forgie me,
I winna lie, come what will o' me)
On ev'ry hand ît will allow'd be,
He's juſt — nae better than he should be.

I readily and freely grant,
He downa see a poor man want;
What's no his ain, he winna tak ît;
What ance he says, he winna break ît;
Ought he can lend he'll no refus't,
Till aft his guidness is abus'd;
And rascals whyles that do him wrang,
Ev'n *that*, he does na mind ît lang:
As Maſter, Landlord, Husband, Father,
He does na fail his part in eîther.

But then, nae thanks to him for a' that;
Nae *godly symptom* ye can ca' that;
It's naething but a milder feature,
Of our poor, sinfu', corrupt Nature:
Ye'll get the beſt o' moral works,
'Mang black *Gentoos*, and Pagan *Turks*,

Or Hunters wild on *Ponotaxi*,
Wha never heard of Orth-d-xy.
That he's the poor man's friend in need,
The GENTLEMAN in word and deed,
It's no through terror of D-mn-t-n;
It's just a carnal inclination,
And Och! that's nae r-g-n-r-t-n!

Morality, thou deadly bane,
Thy tens o' thousands thou hast slain!
Vain is his hope, whase stay an' trust is,
In *moral* Mercy, Truth and Justice!

No—stretch a point to catch a plack;
Abuse a Brother to his back;
Steal thro' the *winnock* frae a wh—re.
But point the Rake that taks the *door*;
Be to the Poor like onie whunstane.
And haud their noses to the grunstane;
Ply ev'ry art o' *legal* thieving;
No matter—stick to *sound believing*.

Learn three-mile pray'rs an' half-mile graces,
Wi' weel spread looves, an' lang, wry faces;
Grunt up a solemn, lengthen'd groan,
And damn a' Parties but your own;
I'll warrant then, ye're nae Deceiver,
A steady, sturdy, staunch *Believer*.

O ye wha leave the springs o' C-lv-n,
For *gumlie dubs* of your ain delvin!
Ye sons of Heresy and Error,
Ye'll *some day* squeel in quaking terror!
When Vengeance draws the sword in wrath,
And in the fire throws the *sheath*;
When Ruin, with his sweeping *besom*,
Juſt frets till Heav'n commission gies him;
While o'er the *Harp* pale Misery moans,
And ſtrikes the ever-deep'ning tones,
Still louder shrieks, and heavier groans!

Your pardon, Sir, for this digression,
I maiſt forgat my *Dedication*;
But when Diviniſy comes cross me,
My readers then are sure to lose me.

So Sir, you see 'twas nae daft vapour,
But I maturely thought iſt proper,
When a' my works I did review,
To *dedicate* them, Sir, to YOU;
Because (ye need na tak iſt ill)
I thought them something like *yoursel*.

Then patronize them wi' your favor,
And your Petitioner shall ever—
I had amaist said, *ever pray*,
But that's a word I need na say:
For prayin I hae little skill o't;
I'm baith dead-sweer, an' wretched ill o't
But I'se repeat each poor man's *pray'r*,
That kens or hears about you, Sir—

'May ne'er Misfortune's gowling bark,
'Howl thro' the dwelling o' the CLERK!
'May ne'er his gen'rous, honest heart,
'For that same gen'rous spirit smart!
'May K******'s far-honor'd name
'Lang beet his hymeneal flame,
'Till H********'s, at least a diz'n,
'Are frae their nuptial labors risen:
'Five bonie Lasses round their table,
'And sev'n braw fellows, stout an' able,
'To serve their King an' Country weel,
'By word, or pen, or pointed steel!
'May Health and Peace, with mutual rays,
'Shine on the ev'ning o' his days;
'Till his wee, curlie *John's* ier-oe,
'When ebbing life nae mair shall flow,
'The last, sad, mournful rites bestow!'

I will not wind a lang conclusion,
With complimentary effusion:
But whilſt your wishes and endeavours,
Are bleſt with Fortune's smiles and favours,
I am, Dear Sir, with zeal moſt fervent,
Your much indebted, humble servant.

But if, which Pow'rs above prevent,
That iron-hearted Carl, *Want*,
Attended, in his grim advances,
By *sad miſtakes*, and *black mischances*,
While hopes, and joys, and pleasures fly him,
Make you as poor a dog as I am,
Your *humble servant* then no more;
For who would humbly serve the Poor?
But by a poor man's hopes in Heav'n!
While recollection's pow'r is giv'n,
If, in the vale of humble life,
The victim sad of Fortune's ſtrife,
I, through the tender-gushing tear,
Should recognise my *Maſter dear*,
If friendless, low, we meet together,
Then, Sir, your hand—my FRIEND and
BROTHER.

TO A

LOUSE

On Seeing one on a Lady's Bonnet at Church

H A! whare ye gaun, ye crowlan ferlie!
    Your impudence protects you fairly:
I canna say but ye ſtrunt rarely,
        Owre *gawze* and *lace*;
Tho' faith, I fear ye dine but sparely,
        On sic a place.

Ye ugly, creepan, blaſtet wonner,
Deteſted, shunn'd, by saunt an' sinner,
How daur ye set your fit upon her,
        Sae fine a *Lady*!
Gae somewhere else and seek your dinner,
        On some poor body.

Swith, in some beggar's haffet squattle;
There ye may creep, and sprawl, and sprattle,
Wi' ither kindred, jumping cattle,
        In shoals and nations;
Whare *horn* nor *bane* ne'er daur unsettle,
        Your thick plantations.

Now haud you there, ye're out o' sight
Below the fatt'rels, snug and tight,
Na faith ye yet! ye'll no be right,
   Till ye've got on it,
The vera tapmost, towrin height
   O' *Miss's bonnet.*

My sooth! right bauld ye set your nose out,
As plump an' gray as onie grozet:
O for some rank, mercurial rozet,
   Or fell, red smeddum,
I'd gie you sic a hearty dose o't,
   Wad dress your droddum!

I wad na been surpriz'd to spy
You on an auld wife's *flainen toy*;
Or aiblins some bit duddie boy,
   On's *wylecoat*;
But Miss's fine *Lunardi,* fye!
   How daur ye do't?

O *Jenny* dinna toss your head,
An' set your beauties a' abread!
Ye little ken what cursed speed
  The blastie's makin!
Thae *winks* and *finger-ends*, I dread,
  Are notice takin!

O wad some Pow'r the giftie gie us
To see oursels as others see us!
It wad frae monie a blunder free us
  An' foolish notion:
What airs in dress an' gait wad lea'e us,
  And ev'n Devotion!

EPISTLE

TO

J . L*****K

AN OLD SCOTCH BARD

April 1ſt 1785

WHILE briers an' woodbines budding green,
 An' Paîtricks scraichan loud at e'en,
And morning Poossie whiddan seen,
  Inspire my Muse,
This freedom, in an *unknown* frien',
  I pray excuse.

 On Faſteneen we had a rockin,
To ca' the crack and weave our ſtockin;
And there was muckle fun and jokin,
  Ye need na doubt;
At length we had a hearty yokin,
  At *sang about.*

There was ae *sang*, amang the reſt,
Aboon them a' it pleas'd me beſt,
That some kind husband had addreſt,
   To some sweet wife:
It thirl'd the heart-ſtrings thro' the breaſt,
   A' to the life.

I've scarce heard ought describ'd sae weel,
What gen'rous, manly bosoms feel;
Thought I, 'Can this be *Pope*, or *Steele*,
   Or *Beattie's* wark;'
They tald me 'twas an odd kind chiel
   About *Muirkirk*.

It pat me fidgean-fain to hear't,
An' sae about him there I spier't;
Then a' that kent him round declar'd,
   He had *ingine*,
That nane excell'd it, few cam near't.
   It was sae fine.

That set him to a pint of ale,
An' either douse or merry tale,
Or rhymes an' sangs he'd made himsel,
   Or witty catches,
'Tween Inverness and Tiviotdale,
   He had few matches.

Then up I gat, an swoor an aith,
Tho' I should pawn my pleugh an' graith,
Or die a cadger pownie's death,
      At some dyke-back,
A *pint* an' *gill* I'd gie them *baith*,
      To hear your crack.

But first an' foremost, I should tell,
Amaist as soon as I could spell,
I to the *crambo-jingle* fell,
      Tho' rude an' rough,
Yet crooning to a body's sel,
      Does weel eneugh.

I am nae *Poet*, in a sense,
But just a *Rhymer* like by chance,
An' hae to Learning nae pretence,
      Yet, what the matter?
Whene'er my Muse does on me glance,
      I jingle at her.

Your Critic-folk may cock their nose,
And say, 'How can you e'er propose,
'You wha ken hardly *verse* frae *prose*,
      'To mak a *sang*?'
But by your leaves, my learned foes,
      Ye're maybe wrang.

What's a' your jargon o' your Schools,
Your Latin names for horns an' ſtools;
If honeſt Nature made you *fools*,
     What sairs your Grammars?
Ye'd better taen up *spades* and *shools*,
     Or *knappin-hammers.*

A set o' dull, conceîted Hashes,
Confuse their brains in *Colledge-classes!*
They *gang in* Stirks, and *come out* Asses;
     Plain truth to speak;
An' syne they think to climb Parnassus
     By dint o' Greek!

Gie me ae spark o' Nature's fire,
That's a' the learning I desire;
Then tho' I drudge thro' dub an' mire
     At pleugh or cart,
My Muse, tho' hamely in attire,
     May touch the heart.

O for a spunk o' ALLAN'S glee,
Or FERGUSON'S, the bauld an' slee,
Or bright L*****K'S, my friend to be,
     If I can hît it!
That would be *lear* eneugh for me,
     If I could get ît.

Now, Sir, if ye hae friends enow,
Tho' *real friends* I b'lieve are few,
Yet, if your catalogue be fow,
   I'se no insist;
But gif ye want ae friend that's true,
   I'm on your list.

I winna blaw about *mysel*,
As ill I like my fauts to tell;
But friends an' folk that wish me well,
   They sometimes roose me;
Tho' I maun own, as monie still,
   As far abuse me.

There's ae *wee faut* they whiles lay to me,
I like the lasses — Gude forgie me!
For monie a Plack they wheedle frae me,
   At dance or fair:
Maybe some *ither thing* they gie me
   They weel can spare.

But MAUCHLINE Race or MAUCHLINE Fair,
I should be proud to meet you there;
We'se gie ae night's discharge to *care*,
   If we forgather,
An' hae a swap o' *rhymin-ware,*
   Wi' ane anither.

The *four-gill chap*, we'se gar him clatter,
An' kirs'n him wi' reekin water;
Syne we'll sit down an' tak our whitter,
  To chear our heart;
An' faith, we'se be *acquainted* better
  Before we part.

Awa ye selfish, warly race,
Wha think that havins, sense an' grace,
Ev'n love an' friendship should give place
  To *catch-the-plack*!
I dinna like to see your face,
  Nor hear your crack.

But ye whom social pleasure charms,
Whose hearts the *tide of kindness* warms,
Who hold your *being* on the terms,
  'Each aid the others,'
Come to my bowl, come to my arms,
  My friends, my brothers!

But to conclude my lang epistle,
As my auld pen's worn to the grissle;
Twa lines frae you wad gar me fissle,
  Who am, most fervent,
While I can either sing, or whissle,
  Your friend and servant.

TO THE SAME

April 21st 1785

WHILE new-ca'd kye rowte at the stake,
  An' pownies reek in pleugh or braik,
This hour on e'enin's edge I take,
      To own I'm debtor,
To honest-hearted, auld L***** K,
      For his kind *letter*.

Forjesket sair, with weary legs,
Rattlin the corn out-owre the rigs,
Or dealing thro' amang the naigs
      Their ten-hours bite,
My awkart Muse sair pleads and begs,
      I would na write.

The tapetless, ramfeezl'd hizzie,
She's saft at best an' something lazy,
Quo' she, 'Ye ken we've been sae busy
      'This month an' mair,
'That trouth, my head is grown right dizzie,
      'An' something sair.'

Her dows excuses pat me mad;
'Conscience,' says I, 'ye thowless jad!
'I'll write, an' that a hearty blaud,
          'This vera night;
'So dinna ye affront your trade,
          'But rhyme it right.

     'Shall bauld L*****K, the *king o' hearts*,
'Tho' mankind were a *pack o' cartes*,
'Roose you sae weel for your deserts,
          'In terms sae friendly,
'Yet ye'll neglect to shaw your parts
          'An' thank him kindly?'

     Sae I gat paper in a blink,
An, down gaed *stumpie* in the ink:
Quoth I, 'Before I sleep a wink,
          'I vow I'll close it;
'An' if ye winna mak it clink,
          'By Jove I'll prose it!'

     Sae I've begun to scrawl, but whether
In rhyme, or prose, or baith thegither,
Or some hotch-potch that's rightly neither,
          Let time mak proof;
But I shall scribble down some blether
          Just clean aff-loof.

My worthy friend, ne'er grudge an' carp,
Tho' Fortune use you hard an' sharp;
Come, kittle up your *moorlan harp*
    Wi' gleesome touch!
Ne'er mind how Fortune *waft* an' *warp*;
    She's but a b—tch.

She's gien me monie a jirt an' fleg,
Sin I could striddle owre a rig;
But by the L—d, tho' I should beg
    Wi' lyart pow,
I'll laugh, an' sing, an' shake my leg,
    As lang's I dow!

Now comes the *sax an' twentieth* simmer,
I've seen the bud upo' the timmer,
Still persecuted by the limmer
    Frae year to year;
But yet, despite the kittle kimmer,
    I, Rob, am here.

Do ye envy the *city-gent*,
Behint a kist to lie an' sklent,
Or purse-proud, big wi' cent per cent,
    An' muckle wame,
In some bit *Brugh* to represent
    A *Baillie's* name?

Or is't the paughty, feudal *Thane*,
Wi' ruffl'd sark an' glancin cane,
Wha thinks himsel nae *sheep-shank bane*,
    But lordly stalks,
While caps an' bonnets aff are taen,
    As by he walks?

'O *Thou* wha gies us each guid gift!
'Gie me o' *wit* an' *sense* a lift,
'Then turn me, if *Thou* please, *adrift*,
    'Thro' Scotland wide;
'Wi' *cits* nor *lairds* I wadna shift,
    'In a' their pride!'

Were this the *charter* of our state,
'On pain o' *hell* be rich an' great,'
Damnation then would be our fate,
    Beyond remead;
But, thanks to *Heav'n*, that's no the gate
    We learn our *creed*.

For thus the royal *Mandate* ran,
When first the human race began,
'The social, friendly, honest man,
    'Whate'er he be,
'Tis *he* fulfils *great Nature's plan*,
    'And none but *he*.'

O *Mandate*, glorious and divine!
The followers o' the ragged Nine,
Poor, thoughtless devils! yet may shine
  In glorious light,
While sordid sons o' Mammon's line
  Are dark as night!

Tho' here they scrape, an' squeeze, an' growl,
Their worthless nievefu' of a *soul*,
May in some *future carcase* howl,
  The forest's fright;
Or in some day-detesting *owl*
  May shun the light.

Then may L*****K and B**** arise,
To reach their native, kindred skies,
And *sing* their pleasures, hopes an' joys,
  In some mild sphere,
Still closer knit in friendship's ties
  Each passing year!

T O

W . S*****N ,
O C H I L T R E E

May — 1785

I GAT your letter, winsome Willie;
    Wi' gratefu' heart I thank you brawlie;
Tho' I maun say't, I wad be silly,
        An' unco vain,
Should I believe, my coaxin billie,
        Your flatterin ſtrain.

    But I'se believe ye kindly meant ît,
I sud be laîth to think ye hinted
Ironic satire, sidelins sklented,
        On my poor Musie;
Tho' in sic phraisin terms ye've penn'd ît,
        I scarce excuse ye.

    My senses wad be in a creel,
Should I but dare a *hope* to speel,
Wi' *Allan,* or wi' *Gilbertfield,*
        The braes o' fame;
Or *Ferguson,* the wrîter-chiel,
        A deathless name.

(O *Ferguson!* thy glorious *parts,*
Ill-suited *law's* dry, musty arts!
My curse upon your whunstane hearts,
   Ye Enbrugh Gentry!
The tythe o' what ye waste at *cartes*
   Wad stow'd his pantry!)

  Yet when a tale comes i' my head,
Or lasses gie my heart a screed,
As whiles they're like to be my dead,
   (O sad disease!)
I kittle up my *rustic reed;*
   It gies me ease.

  Auld COILA, now, may fidge fu' fain,
She's gotten *Bardies* o' her ain,
Chiels wha their chanters winna hain,
   But tune their lays,
Till echoes a' resound again
   Her weel-sung praise.

  Nae *Poet* thought her worth his while,
To set her name in measur'd style;
She lay like some unkend-of isle
   Beside *New Holland,*
Or whare wild-meeting oceans *boil*
   Besouth *Magellan.*

Ramsay an' famous *Ferguson*
Gied *Forth* an' *Tay* a lift aboon;
Yarrow an' *Tweed*, to monie a tune,
  Owre Scotland rings,
While *Irwin*, *Lugar*, *Aire* an' *Doon*,
  Naebody sings.

Th' *Illissus*, *Tiber*, *Thames* an' *Seine*.
Glide sweet in monie a tunefu' line;
But *Willie* set your fit to mine,
  An' cock your crest,
We'll gar our streams an' burnies shine
  Up wi' the best.

We'll sing auld COILA'S plains an' fells,
Her moors red-brown wi' heather bells,
Her banks an' braes, her dens an' dells.
  Where glorious WALLACE
Aft bure the gree, as story tells,
  Frae Suthron billies.

At WALLACE' name, what Scottish blood,
But boils up in a spring-tide flood!
Oft have our fearless fathers strode
  By WALLACE' side,
Still pressing onward, red-wat-shod!
  Or glorious dy'd!

O sweet are COILA'S haughs an' woods,
When lintwhîtes chant amang the buds,
And jinkin hares, in amorous whids,
   Their loves enjoy,
While thro' the braes the cushat croods
   Wîth wailfu' cry!

Ev'n winter bleak has charms to me,
When winds rave thro' the naked tree;
Or frosts on hills of *Ochiltree*
   Are hoary gray;
Or blinding drifts wild-furious flee,
   Dark'ning the day!

O NATURE! A' thy shews an' forms
To feeling, pensive hearts hae charms!
Whether the Summer kindly warms,
   Wi' life an' light,
Or Winter howls, in gusty storms,
   The lang, dark night!

The *Muse* nae *Poet* ever fand her,
Till by himsel he learn'd to wander,
Adown some trottin burn's meander,
   An' no think lang;
O sweet, to stray an' pensive ponder
   A heart-felt sang!

The warly race may drudge an' drive,
Hog-shouther, jundie, ſtretch an' ſtrive,
Let me fair NATURE'S face descrive,
    And I, wi' pleasure,
Shall let the busy, grumbling hive
    Bum owre their treasure.

Fareweel, 'my rhyme-composing' brîther!
We've been owre lang unkenn'd to îther:
Now let us lay our heads thegîther,
    In love fraternal:
May *Envy* wallop in a tether,
    Black fiend, infernal!

While Highlandmen hate tolls an' taxes;
While moorlan herds like guid, fat braxies;
While Terra firma, on her axis,
    Diurnal turns,
Count on a friend, in faîth an' practice,
    In ROBERT BURNS.

POSTSCRIPT

M Y memory's no worth a preen;
 I had amaiſt forgotten clean,
Ye bad me wrîte you what they mean
   By this *new-light*,*
'Bout which our *herds* sae aft hae been
   Maiſt like to fight.

 In days when mankind were but callans,
At *Grammar*, *Logic*, an' sic talents,
They took nae pains their speech to balance,
   Or rules to gie,
But spak their thoughts in plain, braid lallans,
   Like you or me.

 In thae auld times, thy thought the *Moon*,
Juſt like a sark, or pair o' shoon,
Woor by degrees, till her laſt roon
   Gaed paſt their viewin,
An' shortly after she was done
   They gat a new ane.

* A cant-term for those religious opinions, which Dr
TAYLOR of Norwich has defended so ſtrenuously.

This paſt for certain, undisputed;
It ne'er cam i' their heads to doubt ît,
Till chiels gat up an' wad confute ît,
    An' ca'd ît wrang;
An' muckle din there was about ît,
      Baîth loud an' lang.

Some *herds*, weel learn'd upo' the beuk,
Wad threap auld folk the thing miſteuk;
For 'twas the *auld moon* turn'd a newk
    An' out o' sight,
An' backlins-comin, to the leuk.
      She grew mair bright.

This was deny'd, ît was affirm'd;
The *herds* an' *hissels* were alarm'd;
The rev'rend gray-beards rav'd an' ſtorm'd,
    That beardless laddies
Should think they better were inform'd,
      Than their auld dadies.

Frae less to mair ît gaed to ſticks;
Frae words an' aîths to clours an' nicks;
An' monie a fallow gat his licks,
    Wi' hearty crunt;
An' some, to learn them for their tricks,
      Were hang'd an' brunt.

This game was play'd in monie lands
An' *auld-light* caddies bure sic hands,
That faith, the *youngsters* took the sands
    Wi' nimble shanks,
Till *Lairds* forbad, by strict commands,
    Sic bluidy pranks.

But *new-light herds* gat sic a cowe,
Folk thought them ruin'd stick-an-stowe,
Till now amaist on ev'ry *knowe*
    Ye'll find ane plac'd;
An' some, their *New-light* fair avow,
    Just quite barefac'd.

Nae doubt the *auld-light flocks* are bleatan;
Their zealous *herds* are vex'd an' sweatan;
Mysel, I've ev'n seen them greetan
    Wi' girnan spite,
To hear the *Moon* sae sadly lie'd on
    By word an' write.

But shortly they will cowe the louns!
Some *auld-light herds* in neebor towns
Are mind't, in things they ca' *balloons*,
    To tak a flight,
An' stay ae month amang the *Moons*
    An' see them right.

Guid observation they will gie them;
An' when the *auld Moon's* gaun to le'ae them,
The hindmost *shaird*, they'll fetch it wi' them,
    Just i' their pouch,
An' when the *new-light* billies see them,
    I think they'll crouch!

Sae, ye observe that a' this clatter
Is naething but a 'moonshine matter;'
But tho' dull *prose-folk* latin splatter
    In logic tulzie,
I hope we, *Bardies*, ken some better
    Than mind sic brulzie.

EPISTLE

TO

J . R******

ENCLOSING SOME POEMS

O ROUGH, rude, ready-witted R******,
   The wale o' cocks for fun an' drinkin!
There's monie godly folks are thinkin,
   Your *dreams* * an' tricks
Will send you, Korah-like, a sinkin,
   Straught to auld Nick's.

 Ye hae sae monie cracks an' cants,
And in your wicked, druken rants,
Ye mak a devil o' the *Saunts*,
   An' fill them fou;
And then their failings, flaws an' wants,
   Are a' seen thro'.

* A certain humorous *dream* of his was then making a noise in
the world.

Hypocrisy, in mercy spare ît!
That *holy robe*, O dinna tear ît!
Spare't for their sakes wha aften wear ît,
     The lads in *black*;
But your curſt wît, when ît comes near ît,
     Rives't aff their back.

Think, wicked Sinner, wha ye're skaîthing:
It's juſt the *Blue-gown* badge an' claîthing,
O' Saunts; tak that, ye lea'e them naething,
     To ken them by,
Frae ony unregenerate Heathen,
     Like you or I.

I've sent you here, some rhymin ware,
A' that I bargain'd for, an' mair;
Sae when ye hae an hour to spare,
     I will expect,
Yon *Sang* * ye'll sen't, wi' cannie care,
     And no neglect.

* A *Song* he had promised the Author.

Tho' faith, sma' heart hae I to sing!
My Muse dow scarcely spread her wing:
I've play'd mysel a bonie *spring*,
      An' *danc'd* my fill!
I'd better gaen an' sair't the king,
      At Bunker's hill.

'Twas ae night lately, in my fun,
I gaed a rovin wi' the gun,
An' brought a *Paitrick* to the *grun'*,
      A bonie *hen*,
And, as the twilight was begun,
      Thought nane wad ken.

The poor, wee thing was *little hurt*;
I *straiket* it a wee for sport,
Ne'er thinkan they wad fash me for't;
      But, Deil-ma-care!
Somebody tells the *Poacher-Court*,
      The hale affair.

Some auld, us'd hands had taen a note,
That *sic a hen* had got a *shot*;
I was suspected for the plot;
      I scorn'd to lie;
So gat the whissle o' my groat,
      An' pay't the *fee*.

But by my *gun*, o' guns the wale,
An' by my *pouther* an' my *hail*,
An' by my *hen*, an' by her *tail*,
      I vow an' swear!
The *Game* shall Pay, owre moor an' *dail*,
      For this, nieſt year.

As soon's the *clockin-time* is by,
An' the *wee powts* begun to cry,
L—d, I'se hae sportin by an' by,
      For my *gowd guinea*;
Tho' I should herd the *buckskin* kye
      For't, in Virginia!

Trowth, they had muckle for to blame!
'Twas neither broken wing nor limb,
But twa-three *draps* about the *wame*
      Scarce thro' the *feathers*;
An' baith a *yellow George* to claim,
      An' *thole* their *blethers*!

It pits me ay as mad's a hare;
So I can rhyme nor write nae mair;
But *pennyworths* again is fair,
      When time's expedient;
Meanwhile I am, respected Sir,
      Your moſt obedient.

SONG

Tune, Corn rigs are bonie

I

IT was upon a Lammas night,
   When corn rigs are bonie,
Beneath the moon's unclouded light,
   I held awa to Annie:
The time flew by, wi' tentless head,
   Till 'tween the late and early;
Wi' sma' persuasion she agreed,
   To see me thro' the barley.

II

The sky was blue, the wind was still,
   The moon was shining clearly;
I set her down, wi' right good will,
   Amang the rigs o' barley:
I ken't her heart was a' my ain;
   I lov'd her most sincerely;
I kiss'd her owre and owre again,
   Amang the rigs o' barley.

III

I lock'd her in my fond embrace;
    Her heart was beating rarely:
My blessings on that happy place,
    Amang the rigs o' barley!
But by the moon and ſtars so bright
    That shone that night so clearly!
She ay shall bless that happy night,
    Amang the rigs o' barley.

IV

I hae been blythe wi' Comrades dear;
    I hae been merry drinking;
I hae been joyfu' gath'rin gear;
    I hae been happy thinking:
But a' the pleasures e'er I saw,
    Tho' three times doubl'd fairly,
That happy night was worth them a',
    Amang the rigs o' barley.

CHORUS

Corn rigs, an' barley rigs,
    An' corn rigs are bonie:
I'll ne'er forget that happy night,
    Amang the rigs wi' Annie.

SONG

COMPOSED IN AUGUST

Tune, I had a horse, I had nae mair

I

Now westlin winds, and slaught'ring guns
Bring Autumn's pleasant weather;
And the moorcock springs, on whirring wings,
 Amang the blooming heather:
Now waving grain, wide o'er the plain,
 Delights the weary Farmer;
And the moon shines bright, when I rove at night,
 To muse upon my Charmer.

II

The Partridge loves the fruîtful fells;
  The Plover loves the mountains;
The Woodcock haunts the lonely dells;
  The soaring Hern the fountains:
Thro' lofty groves, the Cushat roves,
  The path of man to shun ît;
The hazel bush o'erhangs the Thrush,
  The spreading thorn the Linnet.

III

Thus ev'ry kind their pleasure find,
  The savage and the tender;
Some social join, and leagues combine;
  Some solîtary wander:
Avaunt, away! the cruel sway,
  Tyrannic man's dominion;
The Sportsman's joy, the murd'ring cry,
  The flutt'ring, gory pinion!

IV

But PEGGY dear, the ev'ning's clear,
　　Thick flies the skimming Swallow;
The sky is blue, the fields in view,
　　All fading-green and yellow:
Come let us ſtray our gladsome way,
　　And view the charms of Nature;
The ruſtling corn, the fruîted thorn,
　　And ev'ry happy creature.

V

We'll gently walk, and sweetly talk,
　　Till the silent moon shine clearly;
I'll grasp thy waiſt, and fondly preſt,
　　Swear how I love thee dearly:
Not vernal show'rs to budding flow'rs,
　　Not Autumn to the Farmer,
So dear can be, as thou to me,
　　My fair, my lovely Charmer!

SONG

Tune, Gilderoy

I

FROM thee, ELIZA, I must go,
   And from my native shore:
The cruel fates between us throw
   A boundless ocean's roar;
But boundless oceans, roaring wide,
   Between my love and me,
They never, never can divide
   My heart and soul from thee.

II

Farewell, farewell, ELIZA dear,
   The maid that I adore!
A boding voice is in mine ear,
   We part to meet no more!
But the latest throb that leaves my heart,
   While Death stands victor by,
That throb, ELIZA, is thy part,
   And thine that latest sigh!

THE FAREWELL

TO THE BRETHREN OF ST JAMES'S LODGE, TARBOLTON

Tune, Goodnight and joy be wi' you a'

I

A<small>DIEU</small>! A heart-warm, fond adieu!
  Dear brothers of the *mystic tye*!
Ye favored, *enlighten'd* Few,
  Companions of my social joy!
Tho' I to foreign lands must hie,
  Pursuing Fortune's slidd'ry ba',
With melting heart, and brimful eye,
  I'll mind you still, tho' far awa.

II

Oft have I met your social Band,
  And spent the chearful, festive night;
Oft, honor'd with supreme command,
  Presided o'er the *Sons of light*:
And by that *Hieroglyphic* bright,
  Which none but *Craftsmen* ever saw!
Strong Mem'ry on my heart shall write
  Those happy scenes when far awa!

III

May Freedom, Harmony and Love
 Unîte you in the *grand Design*,
Beneath th' Omniscient Eye above,
 The glorious ARCHITECT Divine!
That you may keep th' *unerring line*,
 Still rising by the *plummet's law*,
Till *Order* bright, completely shine,
 Shall be my Pray'r when far awa.

IV

And *YOU*, farewell! whose merîts claim,
 Juſtly that *higheſt badge* to wear!
Heav'n bless your honor'd, noble Name,
 To MASONRY and SCOTIA dear!
A laſt requeſt, permît me here,
 When yearly ye assemble a',
One *round*, I ask ît wîth a *tear*,
 To him, *the Bard, that's far awa*.

EPITAPH ON A HENPECKED COUNTRY SQUIRE

As father Adam first was fool'd,
    A case that's still too common,
Here lyes a man a woman rul'd,
    The devil rul'd the woman.

EPIGRAM ON SAID OCCASION

O Death, hadst thou but spar'd his life,
    Whom we, this day, lament!
We freely wad exchang'd the *wife*,
    An' a' been weel content.

Ev'n as he is, cauld in his graff
    The *swap* we yet will do't;
Tak thou the Carlin's carcase aff;
    Thou'se get the *saul o' boot.*

ANOTHER

One Queen Artemisa, as old ſtories tell,
When depriv'd of her husband she loved so well,
In respect for the love and affection he'd show'd
 her,
She reduc'd him to duſt, and she drank up
 the Powder.

But Queen N**********, of a diff'rent
  complexion,
When call'd on to order the fun'ral direction,
Would have *eat* her dead lord, on a slender
 pretence,
Not to show her respect, but — *to save the expence*.

EPITAPHS

ON A CELEBRATED RULING ELDER

HERE Sowter **** in Death does sleep;
   To H—ll, if he's gane thither,
Satan, gie him thy gear to keep,
   He'll haud it weel thegither.

ON A NOISY POLEMIC

Below thir stanes lie Jamie's banes;
   O Death, it's my opinion,
Thou ne'er took such a bleth'ran b—tch
   Into thy dark dominion!

ON WEE JOHNIE

Hic jacet wee Johnie

Whoe'er thou art, O reader, know,
   That Death has murder'd Johnie;
An' here his *body* lies fu' low—
   For *saul* he ne'er had ony.

FOR THE AUTHOR'S FATHER

O ye whose cheek the tear of pity ſtains,
    Draw near with pious rev'rence and attend!
Here lie the loving Husband's dear remains,
    The tender Father, and the gen'rous Friend.

The pitying Heart that felt for human Woe;
    The dauntless heart that fear'd no human Pride;
The Friend of Man, to vice alone a foe;
    'For ev'n his failings lean'd to Virtue's side.*'

FOR R.A. Esq

    Know thou, O ſtranger to the fame
Of this much lov'd, much honor'd name!
(For none that knew him need be told)
A warmer heart Death ne'er made cold.

FOR G.H. Esq

The poor man weeps — here G—N sleeps
    Whom canting wretches blam'd:
But with *such as he*, where'er he be,
    May I be *sav'd* or *d—'d*!

* Goldsmith.

A BARD'S EPITAPH

Is there a whim-inspir'd fool,
    Owre faſt for thought, owre hot for rule,
Owre blate to seek, owre proud to snool,
            Let him draw near;
And o'er this grassy heap sing dool,
            And drap a tear.

    Is there a Bard of ruſtic song,
Who, noteless, ſteals the crouds among,
That weekly this area throng,
            O, pass not by!
But with a frater-feeling ſtrong,
            Here, heave a sigh.

    Is there a man whose judgment clear,
Can others teach the course to ſteer,
Yet runs, himself, life's mad career,
            Wild as the wave,
Here pause — and thro' the ſtarting tear,
            Survey this grave.

The poor Inhabîtant below
Was quick to learn and wise to know,
And keenly felt the friendly glow,
     And *softer flame*;
But thoughtless follies laid him low,
     And ſtain'd his name!

Reader attend — whether thy soul
Soars fancy's flights beyond the pole,
Or darkling grubs this earthly hole,
     In low pursuît,
Know, prudent, cautious, *self-controul*
     Is Wisdom's root.

FINIS

AFTERWORD — EFFECT, LEGACY AND PHENOMENON

Kilmarnock saw that first edition of a young man's poems published in 1786 and Burns has not been out of print for a single day since. We are still reading, reciting and enjoying these poems in this two hundred and fiftieth anniversary of the poet's birth. John Cairney's Introduction gives us a perfect insight into the period in which *Poems, Chiefly In the Scottish Dialect* was composed and how it captured the imagination of Burns's countrymen and (of course) his country-women too! This short Afterword hopes to explain how that volume of poetry became the cornerstone of a global phenomenon.

That slight provincial publication was dropped in the small pond of Ayrshire by a man seeking to leave his home, but the ripples that came from that first deliberate action changed Burns's life and have influenced many others of us since. At the time of his death, his poems had been published not just in Kilmarnock, but then in Edinburgh (an expanded edition and a rushed reprint with some notably stinking proof reading), and on to London and (theft being the most profitable form of flattery) in pirate copies in Dublin, Belfast, Philadelphia and New York. There is an irony in RB seeking to raise his fare to escape Scotland for Jamaica by publishing his poems only to find that their success bound him to his homeland in his lifetime. It was in death they spread his fame across the four corners of the world like an Olympic Torch of poetry and hope.

It's a nearly unique phenomenon that a poet, a man of simple upbringing, should become the talisman of Scotland and the Scots (both domestic and displaced) and that the writing, life and character of this Ayrshire ploughman inspire deep human emotion around the globe. I like the burning torch analogy (it could be a Scottish fiery cross, but that symbol is open to mis-interpretation, while RB would be hard pushed to qualify to shelter under the burning bush emblem of the Church of Scotland) for every fire consists of three necessary elements: fuel to build it, a spark to ignite it and oxygen to feed it. What does that mean for RB?

The **fuel** is what you've just been reading – his poems. *The Kilmarnock Edition* (and his subsequent work) enriched us and our language – the poems capture the complexity of man's place as part of, not the master of, creation; of love in its various manifestations and of raw satire – all in the then endangered language of Scots.

The **spark** is the man himself: controversial while alive and the subject of debate and speculation ever since. If poetry is an ability to take complexity and distil it into order, then RB captures the genius of the human soul. His own life however, defies simplicity: the happily married man who has many illegitimate children; a man who refuses payment for contributing Scottish songs to a publisher, but who campaigns for the gift of an excise job, a man who reveres revolutionaries yet loves Scotland's kings, a man equally at home in a bawdy howff or a peeress's salon; and who drank more than was good for him but much less than he claimed. Whatever the kenspeckle clashes, all these warring thoughts and feelings found a touchstone, a centre of gravity in his poems. The spark and the fuel are well matched.

Yet there are many, many poets in the world and, alas, there are likely to be many, many more. Why is it that RB is remembered, honoured, fêted? The reason is the **oxygen** that we seek, the element that feeds the flames. That is the most popular of celebrations – the Burns Supper. No other artist commands a global birthday party in his or her memory, yet from Edinburgh to Dunedin, from Motherwell to Mumbai and seemingly from Ayr to eternity, our poet is actively cheered as is no other literary figure. What makes this phenomenon doubly interesting is that there is no central committee, no founding academy, no pundits or gurus who set these up – it is almost totally spontaneous and in the nicest sense of the word, quite amateur.

The first Burns Supper was held on 21 July 1801 (the fifth anniversary of his death) in Alloway for nine men who knew RB well in his life. His patrons were represented by 'Orator Bob' Aiken (the dedicatee of

'The Cottar's Saturday Night') and former Provost John Ballantine ('The Brigs of Ayr'), while Dr Douglas had found him a job in Jamaica and Mr Crawford had employed RB's late father. The breadth of the community was reflected in the banker, the landowner, the barrackmaster and the rector of Ayr Academy, all friends brought together by a local minister, who was not one of the hellfire clergymen RB railed against, but a man of letters and causes as much as of the cloth, The Rev Hamilton Paul.

Like RB, these nine guests were active Freemasons and the good reverend was inspired by the traditional ritual and practice of the lodge when creating this first celebration – for it was certainly a celebration, not the tearful toast requested by RB in his farewell to the Lodge, for this was a festival dinner not a memorial service.

Paul had a natural flair for party-planning, as the highlights that make up every Supper today all started in that auld clay biggin on that summer's day. Traditional food, introduced by the Grace, with the centrepiece of the menu being a good fat haggis (not yet piped in but definitely Addressed and cut up wi' ready slicht); recitation and communal singing of the works and a profusion of toasts, led by Hamilton Paul's own rhymed first toast to the 'Immortal Memory of Robert Burns' to be greeted fittingly with cheers and toasting 'three times three' as the ritual has it. After Auld Lang Syne had touched the eyes of the assembly, they vowed to meet again – this time on his birthday (although famously they got the date wrong and used 29 January for just over a decade!) and to hold that anniversary feast for all time coming, to pass the flame wider and wider.

Scotland in those days was a mass of clubs and societies. These were mainly local tavern talking shops such as the Crochallan Fencibles who welcomed Burns into their rattlin' roarin' sing-alongs in Edinburgh or like the extraordinarily bawdy Beggars Benison in Anstruther. Many focused on religious developments such as the Poker Club (not the card game but a red hot implement to stir up the faithful) and there were many debating societies (like Tarbolton Bachelors Club, founded by RB). Most of these enjoyed ephemeral success and faced inevitable extinction or at least transformation into the next fad. Yet Burns Clubs, and independent Burns dinners, appeared in ever more places and survived year-on-year – why?

The prototype of all these societies was Freemasonry. Every Scottish town had its lodge under whose roof-trees the rites of old were celebrated in secret by a mix of all classes in local society – in fact, Ayrshire is the home and foundation of Scottish Freemasonry centred on the village of Kilwinning where 'Mother Lodge' resides to this day bearing the unusual serial number in the roll of lodges – Number 0.

This isn't the place to revisit Burns's commitment as a Freemason, or the fraternal support which subscribed to his books and lauded him 'Caledonia's bard' and 'poet laureate'. The important point is that here we have a poet whose philosophy and religion chime in time with the precepts of Freemasonry and where a new festival ritual is encompassed that would have a familiar feel for anyone involved in or merely aware of Masonic tradition. The Burns Supper could be seen as an extra degree of commitment, containing ritual, ceremony, prayer, harmony and fellowship (alcoholic and charitable) so it was a hand-in-glove fit and the Masonic network was the oxygen that fanned the Burns fire.

From Alloway to Ayr then on to a group of Ayrshire-men resident in Greenock in January 1802, the Burns Supper spread using the same Pauline formula. The fire raced through the west coast in the apron pockets of Masonic men – Paisley proudly next (sponsored by the gifted but doomed weaver poet, Tannahill) in 1805 with Kilmarnock, Irvine, Dalry and Dumfries following in short order, each with its claim to have been the stage of a part of the bard's story, each with its aging men in place of honour who knew from personal experience the wonder of RB. Of course, as these festival dinners were in 'Burns Country' the very venues were redolent of the man himself. Not just the iconic Cottage but at Begbie's Inn in Kilmarnock or especially The Globe Inn in Dumfries (his 'favourite 'howff'') – the sign 'Burns Drank Here' remained the mark of a hostelry of good cheer for those early Suppers.

By the time the phenomenon hit Edinburgh, we see a more establishment view – certainly the first dinner in January 1815 saw Hogg the Ettrick Shepherd (and the second poet laureate of Canongate Lodge) give the Immortal Memory, starting a trend into a more open format more akin to what we have today in a subscription dinner event with some with rather grand luminaries in the chair and proposing the toasts – in this case Sir Walter Scott. At this point all Burns Clubs and their festival dinners or suppers were for men only (with the occasional sweet and gracious input from the landlady) and most were closed cells of enthusiasts where the words of our poet were duly celebrated in the proper form – Edinburgh first used invited speakers and paid performers – and although the latter is the more widespread format today, the former still fights its corner.

The first Burns Supper outside Scotland was an expat affair at Oxford University in 1806, with two Glasgow alumni performing the principal roles. That chairman, John Wilson, was to become (as Christopher North) the great columnist of the *Edinburgh Review* and a lifetime Burns orator (though many who heard his orations felt a lifetime had passed before he sat down). The patience of the audience at Magdalen College was not tested that far that night as Samuel McCormick kept to the old fashion of proposing the Immortal Memory in his own rhyme, albeit rather less effective than his hero's verses.

Then, as now, Scots drifted into London for work and 1810 saw the literary chancer Alan Cunningham come from Scotland to London with various plans including capitalising on Burns with a new edition of the works, a project in parallel with the capital's first Burns Supper that year. Over the next 20 years, various small Suppers were held around London but in 1832, under the aegis of the London Burns Club, with the hands of Messrs Wilson and Cunningham in the background, the plan of a grand dinner was formulated, to be held in Freemasons Hall with guest appearances from Lockhart, Hogg and Galt with Robert Burns Jr. and his younger brother James representing the family. As has happened to many an organiser of Suppers since, the plan and its execution drifted apart on the day. Notwithstanding the muddle, and perhaps proving that bad publicity is better than no publicity at all, the event carried on in fits and starts as the first annual festival dinner in London and it still is held today.

Now that the Burns Supper was a fixture across the British Isles, all it took was a fair wind to carry the flames overseas.

Scots had oft looked overseas. In fact, RB wrote 'The Address of Beelzebub' in protest at highlanders being prevented from sailing to find a new life in Canada by their landowners − how the cheviot sheep and 40 years had changed that dynamic. Now through clearance, despair, industrialisation or the desire to find a land where life could be lived to the philosophy of Burns's poems, now many many Scottish families emigrated (with varying degrees of compulsion) to the nascent Empire, boosting the traditional enterprises of trade and soldiering that had seen plenty of Scots spread across the world. With those families came their few saved possessions, a desire to work hard and a hole in the heart where their Scotland sat – that hole could be filled by the verse and song of their own, the poor man's poet, Robert Burns. With those memories and songs came the establishment of Burns clubs and their Burns Suppers across the USA and Canada in the 1820s (notably when John Galt the novelist, cousin of RB and a founder of the Greenock club was working there at that time) and into Australia mainly through merchants and ministers (but no doubt with a few lads with one way tickets paid for by the Courts) who established the first festival in Sydney NSW in 1823, with the first Supper in 1844. These local societies sprang up as the Scots landed and took root in the new countries and their cities.

Some had the additional boost of having a Burns descendent in tow – some officers serving in India had an early Supper in 1812 but the trend only truly prospered through the sub-continent following the Burns sons' service with the East India Company. Similarly, New Zealand benefited from a nephew active in the foundation of Dunedin. The rapid spread of this celebration was primarily seen in the English speaking world, albeit with Scots expat enclaves flying the flag in other regions. However, while Burns and his works were respected by and interested European writers, the celebratory nature failed to expand much beyond the expat pale until in the 20th Century, the growth of communism in Russia and China saw Burns on the curriculum and celebrated as an author of the earth and people whose 'man's a man' lyric echoed the *Internationale* and the Russians, particularly, enjoyed toasting their comrade poet.

Even at this time, when widely spread, the format of the Burns Supper remained pretty true to the original concept. In the expansion abroad, tartan became more important and the ritual became slightly more elaborate — a tradition that continues to this day where haggises are regularly treated like royalty with the armed honour guard, massed pipes and whisky bearers often in the US. It's an understandable desire to honour Scotland's icon with the fond remembered accoutrements of the old homeland. Interestingly, some of those practices have come back to Scotland.

It was not a list of constant successes. The literary festivals of 1844 and the centenaries of birth in 1859 and death in 1896 attracted huge audiences to the fêtes and the dinners and encouraged many more Suppers to be held, but many of the leading Burns Suppers had periods of decay where the organising club fell asleep for sometimes quite long periods. However, for every cancellation there were new festive boards set up in other inns and venues as the practice built the momentum needed to become a tradition.

There were some who opposed lifting a man of such un-Victorian morality on to such a pedestal (and in truth, seeing RB up high can often be the opportunity to see his feet of clay at our own eye level). The temperance movement was very involved, fearing the expansion of the festivities and the associated alcoholic temptation. Add to that the elements in the Kirk that had waited a long time for revenge. The largest and last of the thunderbolts was hurled in 1869, when the Rev Fergus Ferguson railed against the Burns Supper from his Glasgow pulpit in his sermon entitled 'Should Christians Celebrate The Birthday Of Robert Burns?' with the ultra Presbyterian thesis that our poet was an incorrigible atheist and therefore an evil influence on the good folk of Scotland in these golden times of Victorian values. This stirred up a classic controversy in the Scottish press, mostly on the side of defending the positive elements captured at his birthday celebrations. The last word was had by the fount of Victorian values – the Queen herself – who was recorded as dismissing the poor minister's moral crusade by describing her 'fondness' for Burns - thus granting Royal approval to the Burns Supper!

The rate of growth increased from this time and Westminster Abbey even agreed to memorialise RB in Poets Corner in 1885 thanks to the relentless efforts of Colin Rae Brown (one of the most extraordinary

Burnsians from the stock of the Greenock Club). After the service (and in the absence of any enraged thunderbolts from a potentially outraged deity) he and the delegation from Kilmarnock Burns Club agreed to write to all the known clubs to create the Burns Federation – an international institution where clubs could support each other.

The Federation too has its Masonic iconography – London was promised to be No.1 in seniority on the roll of affiliated clubs but Kilmarnock worked a sneaky one and registered itself as Number 0 and Greenock would only consider joining in if recognised as 'Mother Club' – causing the endless feud with Paisley that continues (good naturedly) to rumble on. In true Ayrshire form, Ayr and Alloway felt that such an enterprise was unnecessary as it was (a) new and (b) thought of in Kilmarnock and so did not join until 1908!

Yet even this federation wasn't a centralisation of command and control as even today clubs are affiliated or not according to whim and the payment of a fairly nominal cost. The federation offices are facilitators in modern structure-speak rather than governors. The grass roots is where the action is and the grass roots enjoy the Burns Supper.

There are a number of dissident voices who believe that it is a tradition that does the memory of Burns no favours. The most public critic was Hugh MacDiarmid who provoked the Burns 'fraternity' in uncomprom-

ising terms in famously attacking the content of many
Immortal Memories: 'Mair nonsense has been uttered
in the name of Robert Burns than ony's, barrin' liberty
and Christ'. He believed that the custom of celebrating
Burns had lost the true appreciation of the poetry in
the heady, party mix of tartan, whisky and a raree-show
on his sex life. To this controversy was added some
academic frustration as scholars felt that at many Burns
Suppers, the after dinner speakers state myth as fact,
focus on a few favoured lines from the same poems
every year so that the very format had become the
guardian of a sentimental and trivialised image of
Burns. A third set of critics, less opposed to the
concept of the Supper, became vocal at the social
formality that they felt had crept into the format —
black tie events at expensive hotels seemed out of reach
to the ordinary folk who should be the chief heirs of
RB's legacy.

There is some merit in these arguments, by they are
outweighed by the majority of organisers, speakers and
performers who seek to do justice to the man and to
give honour to his works. Like all fruits of human
endeavour, some work well and some less well. It is a
mistake, however, to assume that every guest at a Burns
Supper has the same knowledge of Burns and so one of
the ways that a good celebration works is to ensure that
the performance of Burns's works and the Immortal
Memory speech in particular is set to inform, educate
and amuse that particular audience, so that each guest

will want to come back for more. And the same holds true for the style of event – one of the interesting trends in the last 10 years is the different ways of presenting the Burns Supper format – not all in starred banqueting halls and full highland dress, but in pubs or restaurants, in family homes or as community events – the popular nature of the Burns Supper means that if you have a critiscm of the style, then you can hold an event next year that challenges whatever point of etiquette or culture you disliked. It's a free world.

And don't forget that each of those dinners, suppers, buffets, lunches or parties follows the Pauline rite of Grace, Haggis, Poems/Songs, Immortal Memory and Auld Lang Syne. Aside from all the tartan banter and quirky traditions, the first nine cronies would recognise the modern Supper as their own. A few changes might seem odd – piping in the haggis (though Paisley still uses a fiddler) and the substitution of the toast to the lassies and its reply for the jumble of dozens of short toasts that prevailed throughout the 19th century. The elderly gentlemen might be a tad shocked to see not only women sitting down to dine but hearing one stand and speak! This nearly universal addition to the Paul programme started off by one of the men thanking the girls in the kitchen for the evening's spread but it started to take off when many clubs allowed ladies to listen from the balcony or gallery in the hall (and over time even take a parallel dinner up there in tartan purdah). Eventually they descended to the level of the male diners (though not in every club yet) and in between the wars claimed the right to ſtand and reply to the Toaſt wìth their own response. It's now an enjoyable tradîtion to have a pair of wìtty speeches where each sex caſts a crîtical eye over the other. I think RB would have approved.

But other than that, ìt's an unbroken and spontaneous line from Burns Cottage in 1801. Here is a celebration wîthout parallel in the world which is dedicated to our Poet whose works speak to us as clearly today as they did to the nine men who heard the poems from the poet's own mouth.

So from 612 copies on 31 July 1786 to millions of copies in a hoſt of languages in myriad countries – not bad for a lad frae Kyle.

More people celebrate the life of Burns each January – whether at a formal Burns Supper, or juſt informally around their own kîtchen table – than populated Scotland the day he died. The power of his verses to move our hearts is unqueſtioned, but the unique spread of Burns and his works is a direct function of good old Hamilton Paul and his Masonic ringmaſter's skills which created a way in which people can participate in the poems and the man himself and hopefully walk away at the end both happier and wiser.

The Burns Supper is like haggis, there are good ones and bad ones, and some cannot abide ìt at any price. Some now are corporate affairs wìth a token nod to Burns, some are weighed down by the dust of ages, sometimes the speakers aren't clever, sometimes the food is cold, sometimes the drink runs out (horrible to contemplate…) but a well planned Burns Supper — with the unique balance of conviviality, pride and being touched by the words of a great man and a wondrous poet — is impossible to surpass. All you have to do is

1   Address a haggis (it is polite to try and eat a wee bit)

2   Sing his songs and recite his poems (or have someone do it for you)

3   Toast his Immortal Memory (and it needn't even be in whisky!)

with as much or as little formal structure, dress or ritual as your guests want. It is quite simply the best party in the world. That, because of the unique spirit of this great man, is why the celebration of his life and loves, his wit and works is shared by people the world over and will be for the next 250 years.

All that came from this little book, *Poems, Chiefly in the Scottish Dialect* — read it again and join in the celebration. I'll see you at the next Burns Supper.

Clark McGinn
President of The Burns Club of London, number 1 on the roll of the World Burns Federation.
www.worldburnsclub.com

GLOSSARY

WORDS that are universally known, and those that differ from the English only by the elision of letters by apoſtrophes, or by varying the termination of the verb, are not inserted. The terminations may be thus known; the participle present, inſtead of *ing*, ends, in the Scotch Dialect, in *an* or *in*; in *an*, particularly, when the verb is composed of the participle present, and any of the tenses of the auxiliary, *to be*. The paſt time and participle paſt are usually made by shortening the *ed* into *'t*.

A

ABACK, behind, away
Abiegh, at a diſtance
Ae, one
Agley, wide of the aim
Aiver, an old horse
Aizle, a red ember
Ane, one, an
Ase, ashes
Ava, at all, of all
Awn, the beard of oats, &c.

B

BAIRAN, baring
Banie, bony
Baws'nt, having a whîte ſtripe down the face
Ben, *but and ben*, the country kîtchen and parlour
Bellys, bellows
Bee, *to let bee*, to leave in quiet
Biggin, a building
Bield, shelter
Blaſtet, worthless
Blather, the bladder
Blink, a glance, an amorous leer, a short space of time
Blype, a shred of cloth, &c.

Booſt, behoved
Brash, a sudden illness
Brat, a worn fhred of Cloth
Brainge, to draw unſteadily
Braxie, a morkin sheep
Brogue, an affront
Breef, an invulnerable charm
Breaſtet, sprung forward
Burnewin, *q.d.* burn the wind, a Blacksmîth.

C

CA', to call, to drive
Caup, a small, wooden dish wîth two lugs, or handles
Cape ſtane, cope ſtone
Cairds, tinkers
Cairn, a loose heap of ſtones
Chuffie, fat-faced
Collie, a general and sometimes a particular name for country curs
Cog, or **coggie**, a small wooden dish wîthout handles
Cootie, a pretty large wooden dish
Crack, conversation, to converse
Crank, a harsh, grating sound
Crankous, fretting, peevish

Croon, a hollow, continued moan

Crowl, to creep

Crouchie, crook-backed

Cranreuch, the hoar frost

Curpan, the crupper

Cummock, a short staff

D

DAUD, the noise of one falling flat, a large piece of bread, &c.

Daut, to caress, to fondle

Daimen, now and then, seldom

Daurk, a day's labour

Deleeret, delirious

Dead-sweer, very loath, averse

Dowie, crazy and dull

Donsie, unlucky, dangerous

Doylte, stupified, hebetated

Dow, am able

Dought, was able

Doyte, to go drunkenly or stupidly

Drummock, meal and water mixed raw

Drunt, pet, pettish humor

Dush, to push as a bull, ram, &c

Duds, rags of clothes

E

EERIE, frighted; particularly the dread of spirits

Eldritch, fearful, horrid, ghastly

Eild, old age

Eydent, constant, busy.

F

FA', fall, lot

Fawsont, decent, orderly

Faem, foam

Fatt'rels, ribband ends, &c.

Ferlie, a wonder, to wonder; also a term of contempt

Fecht, to fight

Fetch, to stop suddenly in the draught, and then come on too hastily

Fier, found, healthy

Fittie lan' the near horse of the hindmost pair in the plough

Flunkies, livery servants

Fley, to frighten

Fleesh, fleece

Flisk, to fret at the yoke

Flichter, to flutter

Forbears, ancestors

Forby, besides

Forjesket, jaded

Fow, full, drunk; a bushel, &c.

Freath, froath

Fuff, to blow intermittedly

Fyle, to dirty, to foil

G

GASH, wise, sagacious, talkative; to converse

Gate, or gaet, way, manner, practice

Gab, the mouth; to speak boldly

Gawsie, jolly, large

Geck, to toss the head in pride or wantonness

Gizz, a wig

Gilpey, a young girl

Glaizie, smooth, glittering

Glunch a frown; to frown

Glint, to peep

Grushie, of thick, stout growth

Gruntle, the visage; a grunting noise

Grousome, loathsomely grim

H

HAL, or hald, hold, biding place

Hath, a term of contempt
Haverel, a quarter-wit
Haurl, to drag, to peel
Hain, to save, to spare
Heugh, a crag, a coal-pit
Hecht, to forebode
Hiftie, dry, chapt, barren
Howe, hollow
Hoste or Hoast, to cough
Howk, to dig
Hoddan, the motion of a sage
country farmer on an old cart
   horse
Houghmagandie, a species of
   gender composed of the
   masculine and feminine united
Hoy, to urge incessantly
Hoyte, a motion between a trot
   and a gallop
Hogshouther, to justle with the
   shoulder

I

ICKER, an ear of corn
Ier-oe, a great grand child
Ingine, genius
Ill-willie, malicious, unkind

J

JAUK, to dally at work
Jouk, to stoop
Jocteleg, a kind of knife
Jundie, to justle

K

KAE, a daw
Ket, a hairy, ragged fleece of wool
Kiutle, to cuddle, to caress, to
   fondle
Kiaugh, carking anxiety
Kirsen, to christen

L

LAGGEN, the angle at the
   bottom of a wooden dish
Laithfu', bashful
Leeze me, a term of
   congratulatory endearment
Leal, loyal; true
Loot, did let
Lowe, flame; to flame
Lunt, smoke; to smoke
Limmer, a woman of easy virtue
Link, to trip along
Lyart, grey
Luggie, a small, wooden dish with
   one handle

M

MANTEELE, a mantle
Melvie, to foil with meal
Mense, good breeding
Mell, to meddle with
Modewurk, a mole
Moop, to nibble as a sheep
Muslin kail, broth made up
   simply of water, barley and
   greens

N

NOWTE, black cattle
Nieve, the fist

O

OWRE, over
Outler, lying in the fields, not
   housed at night

P

PACK, intimate, familiar
Pang, to cram
Painch, the paunch
Paughty, proud, saucy

Pattle or pettle, the ploughſtaff
Peghan, the crop of fowls, the
 ſtomach
Penny-wheep, small beer
Pine, pain, care
Pirratch, or porrîtch, pottage
Pliskie, trick
Primsie, affectedly nice
Prief, proof

Q
QUAT, quiſt, did quiſt
Quaikin, quaking

R
RAMFEEZL'D, overspent
Raep or rape, a rope
Raucle, ſtout, clever
Raible, to repeat by rote
Ram-ſtam, thoughtless
Raught, did reach
Reeſtet, shrivelled
Reeſt, to be reſtive
Reck, to take heed
Rede, counsel, to counsel
Ripp, a handful of unthreshed
 corn, &c.
Rief, reaving
Risk, to make a noise like the
 breaking of small roots wîth the
 plough
Rowt, to bellow
Roupet, hoarse
Runkle, a wrinkle
Rockin, a meeting on a winter
 evening

S
SAIR, sore
Saunt, a saint

Scrimp, scant; to ſtint
Scriegh, to cry shrilly
Scrieve, to run smoothly and
 swiftly
Screed, to tear
Scawl, a Scold
Sconner, to loath
Sheen, bright
Shaw, a lîttle wood; to show
Shaver, a humorous mischievous
 wag
Skirl, a shrill cry
Sklent, to slant, to fib
Skiegh, mettlesome, fiery, proud
Slype, to fall over like a wet furrow
Smeddum, powder of any kind
Smytrie, a numerous collection of
 small individuals
Snick-drawing, trick-contriving
Snash, abusive language
Sowther, to cement, to solder
Splore, a ramble
Spunkie, fiery; will o' wisp
Spairge, to spurt about like water
 or mire, to soil
Sprîttie, rushy
Squatter, to flutter in water
Staggie, diminutive of Stag
Steeve, firm
Stank, a pool of ſtanding water
Stroan, to pour out like a spout
Stegh, to cram the belly
Stibble-rig, the reaper who takes
 the lead
Sten, to rear as a horse
Swîth, get away
Syne, since, ago, then

T

TAPETLESS, unthinking

Tawie, that handles quietly

Tawted, or tawtet, matted together

Tact, a small quantity

Tarrow, to murmur at one's
allowance

Thowless, slack, pithless

Thack an' raep, all kinds of
necessaries, particularly clothes

Thowe, thaw

Tirl, to knock gently, to uncover

Toyte, to walk like old age

Trashtrie, trash

W

Wauket, thickened as fullers do
cloth

Water-kelpies, a sort of
mischievous spirits that are said
to haunt fords, &c.

Water-brose, brose made simply
of meal and water

Wauble, to swing

Wair, to lay out, to spend

Whaizle, to wheez

Whisk, to sweep

Wintle, a wavering, swinging
motion

Wiel, a small whirlpool

Winze, an oath

Wonner, wonder, a term of
contempt

Wooer-bab, the garter knotted
below the knee with a couple of
loops and ends

Wrack, to vex, to trouble

Y

YELL, dry, spoken of a cow

Ye, is frequently used for the
singular

Young guidman, a new married
man

ALSO PUBLISHED BY LUATH PRESS

The Merry Muses of Caledonia by Robert Burns, edited by
Valentina Bold and illustrated by Bob Dewar

On the Trail of Robert Burns by John Cairney

*Immortal Memories — A Compilation of Toasts to the Immortal
Memory of Robert Burns as delivered at Burns Suppers around the
world together with other orations, verses and addresses 1801—2001*
by John Cairney

Burnscripts by John Cairney

The Luath Burns Companion introduced and edited by
John Cairney

*Burnsiana — Artworks and Poems Inspired by the Life and Legacy of
Robert Burns* by Calum Colvin and Rab Wilson

The Ultimate Burns Supper Book by Clark McGinn

*As Others See Us — Personal views on the life and works of Robert
Burns*, with photographic portraits by Tricia Malley and
Ross Gillespie

Kate o Shanter's Tale and other Poems by Matthew Fitt

Between Ourselves (a novel based on the life and loves of
Robert Burns) by Donald Smith

Luath Press Limited

committed to publishing well written books worth reading

LUATH PRESS takes its name from Robert Burns, whose little collie Luath (*Gael.*, swift or nimble) tripped up Jean Armour at a wedding and gave him the chance to speak to the woman who was to be his wife and the abiding love of his life. Burns called one of 'The Twa Dogs' Luath after Cuchullin's hunting dog in Ossian's *Fingal*. Luath Press was established in 1981 in the heart of Burns country, and now resides a few steps up the road from Burns' first lodgings on Edinburgh's Royal Mile.

Luath offers you distinctive writing with a hint of unexpected pleasures.

Most bookshops in the UK, the US, Canada, Australia, New Zealand and parts of Europe either carry our books in stock or can order them for you. To order direct from us, please send a £sterling cheque, postal order, international money order or your credit card details (number, address of cardholder and expiry date) to us at the address below. Please add post and packing as follows: UK – £1.00 per delivery address; overseas surface mail – £2.50 per delivery address; overseas airmail – £3.50 for the first book to each delivery address, plus £1.00 for each additional book by airmail to the same address. If your order is a gift, we will happily enclose your card or message at no extra charge.

Luath Press Limited
543/2 Castlehill
The Royal Mile
Edinburgh EH1 2ND
Scotland
Telephone: 0131 225 4326 (24 hours)
email: sales@luath.co.uk
Website: www.luath.co.uk

ILLUSTRATION: IAN KELLAS